ARCHITECTU[RE]
VISIONS THE DRAW[INGS OF] HUGH FERRISS

ARTIST AT WORK, 1925

Hugh Ferriss in his penthouse studio at the Architect's Building in New York, applying the finishing touches to a "Street Vista of the Future" that shows airplanes swooping in for an aerial landing atop skyscrapers. At center is a "Maximum Mass" zoning study, next to a view of pyramidal structures entitled "The Clay Emerging into Practical Form." The haloed skyscraper at far left was described by Ferriss as "a great tower to which dirigibles will be moored and down the sides of which will run escalators for passengers of the air" (a description that recalls Antonio Sant 'Elia's *Manifesto of Futurist Architecture* of 1914). These mural-size drawings, photographically enlarged from preliminary sketches and painted over by the artist and others, were exhibited that year as "A Vision of the Titan City, 1975" in a Tercentenary Pictorial Pageant of New York that took place in October 1925.

ARCHITECTURAL VISIONS
THE DRAWINGS OF HUGH FERRISS

BY JEAN FERRISS LEICH // WITH AN ESSAY BY PAUL GOLDBERGER // FOREWORD BY ADOLF PLACZEK

WHITNEY LIBRARY OF DESIGN
AN IMPRINT OF WATSON-GUPTILL PUBLICATIONS/NEW YORK

To Ellen and Christopher

First published 1980 in New York by Whitney Library of Design,
an imprint of Watson-Guptill Publications,
a division of Billboard Publications, Inc.,
1515 Broadway, New York, N.Y. 10036

Library of Congress Cataloging in Publication Data
Leich, Jean Ferriss, 1920–
    Architectural visions.
    Bibliography: p.
    1. Ferriss, Hugh, 1889–   2. Architects—
United States—Biography. I. Ferriss, Hugh,
1889–   II. Title.
NA737.F47L44   720′ .92′4 [B] 79-27409
ISBN 0-8230-7054-9

Manufactured in U.S.A.

First Printing, 1980

Paperback Edition 1986
ISBN 0-8230-7055-7

ACKNOWLEDGMENTS

The preparation of this book was made possible by an Arnold Brunner Scholarship award from the New York chapter of the American Institute of Architects. For advice and encouragement at various stages of the project, special thanks are due to individual members of the Brunner committee; to Ada Louise Huxtable, member of the editorial board of *The New York Times*, whose comments have provided inspiration; to Catha Grace Rambusch, executive director of The Committee for Preservation of Architectural Records; to architect Walter H. Kilham, Jr.; and to Adolf K. Placzek, Librarian, and Janet Parks, Archivist, at Avery Library, Columbia University. Finally, I must express special gratitude to those colleagues and friends of Hugh Ferriss who so generously responded to my requests for advice and information, especially architects Max Abramovitz and Wallace K. Harrison, who over the years employed Ferriss to delineate so many of the important projects with which he himself was associated from Rockefeller to Lincoln Center.

The rendering is a means toward an end;
the end is architecture.
Hugh Ferriss, 1940

CONTENTS

Tower of Water and Light,
Chicago Exposition, 1933.

LIST OF DRAWINGS

FOREWORD

I N THE FOLLOWING pages an extraordinary figure will emerge in his full dimension: Hugh Ferriss (1889–1962), architect, architectural renderer, city planner, and utopian. His vision of the modern city and his ability to translate vast projects into dramatic but clear-cut images exercised an enormous influence on the architects and the architecture of his generation. He produced two books which conveyed both the vision and the ability: *The Metropolis of Tomorrow* of 1929 and *Power of Buildings* of 1953. They are long out of print, and to the public of a later generation Hugh Ferriss has become a somewhat remote, an almost enigmatic figure. Now, thanks to the devotion and scholarship of Jean Leich, Ferriss's daughter, the present volume will make the outstanding drawings from these books as well as many others available and will also bring the man, the artist with his breath-taking technique and the eloquence of his ideas, into focus.

Hugh Ferriss, born in St. Louis and trained in architecture at Washington University, came to New York in 1912. He was to spend all his life in that Metropolis (if not Of Tomorrow, then certainly of his day). His first employment as an architect was with Cass Gilbert, the designer of the Woolworth Building, the first of the great New York skyscrapers. It was the skyscraper, in fact, which remained at the center of Ferriss's vision throughout his life—not the Gothic skyscraper of Gilbert (of which he was critical), nor even Louis Sullivan's subtle and decorative office buildings, but the bare, soaring, dramatic skyscrapers of the twenties and thirties: not cathedrals of commerce, but structures of material progress and power.

After 1915, Hugh Ferriss was on his own. He turned from architectural practice to architectural rendering, where his genius lay, and soon became the country's most sought-after and successful renderer.

The question is often asked what an architectural rendering is. In his authoritative article "Rendering, Architectural" for the *Encyclopaedia Britannica* of 1929 and subsequent editions Ferriss defines it as follows: "Architectural rendering is a pictorial art whose subject is to visualize architectural conceptions. . . ."

But, of course, that is not all. As Ferriss goes on to say, rendering really has six objectives: ". . . the first three have long been recognized: to convey advance realisations of proposed structures, to aid in crystallizing ideas in the architect's mind and to interpret the architectural significance of existing structures. The other three remain largely for future development: to serve as criterion and guide in city planning, to assist in evolving new types of architecture and to strengthen the psychological influence of architecture on human values. . . ."

Here is expressed what made Ferriss, who succeeded in all six, such a great figure—and also what makes him of such abiding interest. His art served not only the realization of great projects (he was involved in the major ones: Rockefeller Center, the UN in its various design phases, and finally Lincoln Center); but he was also intensely concerned with a vision of the future, the emerging highrise city—not as in Le Corbusier's concept of the dispersed, loosely organized *Ville Radieuse*, but as a dense, compact, power-full organism. The arrangement of the material in this book is therefore most apt: two parts, one dealing with "Dreams," the other with "Realities": dreams which were not fantasies but concrete proposals, possible solutions, future realities; and realities of great buildings which assume the dreamlike shapes of artistic, pictorial experience. Ferriss himself organized his first and greatest book, *The Metropolis of Tomorrow*, along similar lines: part one is called Cities of Today, part two was Projected Trends, including such specific urbanistic ideas as "pedestrian over wheel traffic," apartments on bridges, hanging gardens, and of course the all-important stepback building. The third part is all dreams: Night in the Science Zone, Vista in the Art Zone, symbolic complexes for Power, Finance, Technology, Religion, and Philosophy.

In all of this, there is the sheer beauty of the architectural drawings themselves. Not since Piranesi has architectural draftsmanship been used with such stunning visual effect. But Piranesi—with whom Ferriss has occasionally been compared—was looking backward for inspiration: to the ruins of Roman antiquity above all. And there was the vast gloom of his imaginary prisons. As Ferriss had little use for historic forms, he looked into the future. He drew, as works of art and as an artist, dams, bridges, silos, skyscrapers. Unlike Piranesi, he perceived them—to use Wölfflin's terms—as painterly forms rather than linear patterns, as masses and volumes, darkness and light rather than as lines, points, and hatched planes. Possibly, this is why he preferred the soft pencil, charcoal and crayon to the hard edge of pen and ink.

When considering the utopian side of Ferriss's genius, it is the visionary architects of the French Revolution who come to mind: above all Claude-Nicholas Ledoux (1736-1806) who in a grandiose scheme proposed a whole new city, la Ville de Chaux. His drawings, as well as those of his contemporaries Lequeu and Boullée, share something of the fantastic and progressive spirit of Ferriss. However, none of Lequeu's or Boullée's schemes, nor la Ville de Chaux itself, was ever realized, while Ferriss's ideas on city planning and his renderings for major architectural projects had the closest connection with what was actually happening or was about to happen.

As if all the hidden drama of his drawings wanted out in words too, there comes a point, almost suddenly, when Ferriss breaks into pure poetry.

Buildings like crystals.
Walls of translucent glass.
Sheer glass blocks sheathing a steel grill.
No Gothic branch: no Acanthus leaf: no recollection of the plant world.
A mineral kingdom.
Gleaming stalagmites.
Forms as cold as ice.
Mathematics.
Night in the Science Zone.

This could have been written by a German Expressionist or a Russian Constructivist after 1917, a Bruno Taut, or a Tatlin. It is another facet of Hugh Ferriss's truly modern sensibility—a sensibility which once again shines through the pages of this book with undiminished vigor and magic.

Adolf K. Placzek

E S S A Y S

HUGH FERRISS:

By Jean Ferriss Leich

LOOKING BACK on his long career as an architectural delineator and designer, it is easy to see that Hugh Ferriss and his central subject, the great American skyscraper, were contemporaries. In 1889, the year of the artist's birth, the Auditorium Building opened in Chicago—the first important project completed by Louis Sullivan, the founder of the Chicago School of modern American architecture. By 1903, when Ferriss entered preparatory school in his hometown of St. Louis,[1] the center of action in urban building had begun to shift eastward, and by the time he arrived in New York ten years later, the foundations for the skyscraper boom of the 1920s were firmly in place.

Although trained as an architect, he decided early on to draw, rather than to construct, buildings, entering the narrow field of architectural rendering: "A branch of pictorial art and of architectural design," as he later defined it for the *Encyclopaedia Britannica*, "whose special aim is to show, before buildings have been built, how they will look after they have been built."[2] Technical virtuosity, coupled with a soaring imagination, propelled him to the top of his profession. By the mid-1920s he was not only America's best-known delineator of the contemporary city, but also her most persuasive prophet of the city yet to come. City planners sought his advice; students gathered in classrooms to hear him speak and made pilgrimages to his penthouse studio to watch him at work. Building-product manufacturers commissioned him to advertise their wares; management firms displayed his work as bait to lure prospective tenants.[3] Ferriss renderings were shown in exhibitions here and abroad and published in professional journals and in the daily press.

Of all his clients, however, it was the architectural community itself that most admired his drawings, not only for their success in attracting financial support for proposed building projects, but also because his designs provided a forecast of the future. To leading New York architects, visualizations by Ferriss were logical projections of their own ideas and plans. A "new epoch in architecture," as Ferriss described it in 1922, seemed just around the corner.[4] By the end of the decade, "No other interpretation of the modern American skyscrapers," stated *The Christian Science Monitor*, "so clearly defines their issues and possibilities as that of Hugh Ferriss."[5]

That he was able to expand the role of the professional delineator to that of "U.S. architecture's most grandiose seer"[6] was due, in part, to the optimistic spirit of the age. However, it was his prowess as a draftsman that gave him a unique place in the architectural establishment of the day. Ever since he first came to public attention in 1918, his work has been praised as massive, romantic, powerful, and dramatic. For Adolf Placzek, director of the Avery Library at Columbia University, Ferriss renderings come closer than any others of this century to capturing the "power and compelling fascination of unlimited space" that also characterized the output, 200 years ago, of the Italian master draftsman, Giovanni Battista

INTRODUCTION

Piranesi.[7] That likeness was noted so frequently by reviewers over the years that the *Architectural Forum* once referred to Piranesi as "the 18th-century Hugh Ferriss."[8]

As a licensed architect and "design consultant"—the term that he himself preferred to describe his role—Ferriss's work embraced a wide variety of activities concerned with architectural design, from projecting, in the '20s, proposals of his own for cities of the future to interpreting, in the '40s, plans put forward by multimembered boards of design. Although often described as an "illustrator," the word may be applied to Ferriss only if one recalls that he was an illustrator not so much of buildings as of monumental forms and their relationships in space. Mountains and pyramids, dams and skyscrapers, all struck a responsive chord in him, and in drawing them he was primarily concerned with basic structure and mass. The essentially abstract nature of his work is most evident, perhaps, in renderings of imaginary subjects, but it is true as well of all his best drawings of actual buildings, in which surface detail is modified, or even discarded altogether. Although his technique has been decried, on occasion, as "blurred" and "ambiguous" (on the assumption that it sprang from a desire to mask or distort architectural reality[9]), Ferriss himself maintained that his intention was to expose, not suppress, the truth of the building as he saw it: ". . . the underlying truth of a building is that it is a Mass in Space. . . . I usually, as a first step, put down some light lines or tones which suggest (to me, as I am drawing) the existence of the three dimensions of Space. By gradually increasing the definition of these lines . . . I produce, to my own mind, the illusion of forming Mass within this Space. . . . In general, I fancy the finished result as emerging gradually, and as a whole, from the background."[10]

A contemporary delineator, Ernest Burden, defines the renderer's craft: "There are two kinds of renderers: those interested in giving a faithful representation of what a building will look like, and those interested in presenting a total artistic vision. Drawings by Hugh Ferriss belong in the last category. They are expressions of architectural concepts, rather than portrayals of how a building will look. In his work, drawing and design are inseparable."[11]

U NLIKE THOSE artists who are content to be seen but not heard, Ferriss was an articulate writer and speaker, and the author of two books illustrating contemporary trends in American architecture: *The Metropolis of Tomorrow* published in 1929 and *Power in Buildings* of 1953. The most revealing account, however, of the artist's own view of the purpose and practice of his craft was given in an article on architectural rendering written in 1929 for the *Encyclopaedia Britannica*, where it continued to appear, with revisions, until 1973.

Of the two words "architectural" and "rendering," the first, Ferriss

Rendering: "An Exercise in Imagination"

wrote, is by far the most important; rendering should be regarded merely as a means "to help get projects designed; to help get the designs understood by all concerned, and thereby to help get buildings built."[12] To this end, the professional delineator employs two principal tools: the preliminary design study and the final presentation rendering, showing the proposed structure as it will appear when completed. The aim of the former, which may be no more than a thumbnail sketch, is to help crystallize the original plan in the mind of the architect himself (as Ferriss noted, "not all architects who design well can draw well"[13]), while that of the latter is to provide a preview of the proposed structure for the architect's client, who wants to know what he will get for his money. Ferriss was much in demand for his presentation renderings, but he especially enjoyed the preliminary design sketch. He was forever laying out imaginary plans, not only at his drawing board, but on any surface that might come to hand. Some of his best ideas were first outlined with pencil or fork on a tablecloth in the dining room of The Architectural League of New York, which then occupied a pair of converted townhouses on East 40th Street, just around the corner from Ferriss's rooftop studio in the Architect's Building, 101 Park Avenue. Few who knew the artist will forget the ease with which he could turn out plans and perspectives, talking as he drew, eyes half-closed against the smoke of an ever-present cigarette.

For Ferriss, his art's chief problem constituted its principal attraction: that of preparing a "reliable" drawing of the proposed building, conveying a "lively sense" of its reality, at a time when the structure itself is only a gleam in the architect's eye. "For to portray the proposed building is to portray something that does not exist; rendering is an exercise in imagination. But if a picture is to be other than an architectural fantasy, or better than an architectural fake, the imagination must be fully controlled by a realization of the structural facts involved. It is a matter of equating artistic reach to architectural grasp."[14]

The greatest accuracy in the world, Ferriss argued, will not in itself convey the complex impression that a building makes upon the eye and mind of the beholder: The truthful rendering must be a synthesis not only of structural, but of emotional and intellectual facts. The draftsman must consider his subject as an assemblage of structural parts, resting firmly on the ground, but this is only the beginning of his task. The atmosphere that modifies the building should be suggested as well, in texture and color, in light and shade. Another demanding aspect of the delineator's art is implying in a single, fixed image the composite impression received by the passerby. Viewed in this way, any building is an object in motion. All this, however, is a prelude to the renderer's most important aim: portraying the psychological content of the subject. Buildings, Ferriss said, "possess an individual existence . . . now dynamic, now serene," and it is the duty of the delineator, as of any conscientious portraitist, to be alert to the "emotional tone, the particular mood" of his subject. In such "outlying psychological domains," rendering, "like the other arts, may attain its happiest freedom of movement."

In 1925, Ferriss summarized the renderer's task: "to serve as criterion and guide in city planning, to assist in evolving new types of architecture, and to strengthen the psychological influence of architecture on human values."[15]

A Beaux-Arts Beginning

ALTHOUGH architectural drawing has recently regained some of its former luster—in the eyes, at least, of museum curators and collectors of art—it has become primarily a self-taught skill. The very existence of so-called rendering factories, in which teams of specialists work assembly-line fashion to produce a final, composite drawing, implies a complete turnabout from drawing's place in the early 1900s.[16] In those days, expert draftsmanship was a part of every architect's education, an essential tool to be used in a certain, prescribed way, and then only after long and careful training.

Like most architects of his generation, Ferriss's education stemmed from the Ecole des Beaux-Arts in Paris, which students absorbed either at the source or in one of the American schools of architecture that sprang up before the turn of the century.[17] In 1906, his first year at Washington University, that school of architecture was one of the newest and best west of the Mississippi. Here, under Paris-trained instructors of design—a subject that formed the mainstay of the Beaux-Arts curriculum—the 17-year-old and his classmates were introduced to the "broad, unchangeable principles of architecture illustrated by the monuments of past ages."[18] Following the example of their counterparts in Paris, the students progressed through a series of *projects* in ascending order of difficulty; starting with detailed studies of the Greek and Roman orders painstakingly copied from plaster casts in the school museum, they advanced to such problems in design as: "A chapel screen in the Gothic style, an open timber ceiling in the Italian Renaissance style or the portal of a fortress with appropriate treatment in the Tuscan order."[19]

Although Ferriss traced an early bias toward architecture back to a picture of the Parthenon received on his fifth birthday, he did not as a student share the American awe of historical styles that produced the Chicago World's Columbian Exposition of 1893. Growing up in St. Louis, he saw Louis Sullivan's Wainwright Building of 1890 as a strong contender to the office building of traditional design. While still at the university, he journeyed to Buffalo, New York, expressly to sketch the "powerful and forthright mass" of the Larkin Building, completed a few years before by Frank Lloyd Wright. One of the "greatest puzzles of architectural education," in his later view, was the fact that he and his fellow students were "directed for artistic inspiration not to the field or the laboratory but to the library—not to vital function but to historic precedent."[20] In 1911, graduating as one of six students to receive a Bachelor of Science degree in architecture—at that time and place the highest offered in his field—Ferriss was impatient with the classical models set before him. It was time, he thought, to stop imitating the past and look to the future.

The City and the Skyscraper

In 1912, after a year as junior draftsman with the St. Louis architects, Mariner and LaBeaume, Ferriss found a place in the New York office of Cass Gilbert, where he was put to work drawing details of the Woolworth Building, then under construction. Under the guidance of Tom Johnson, Gilbert's chief designer, Ferriss and his fellow apprentices received a thorough practical training, the best that the city had to offer, working out every facet of the great Gothic tower as it rose to an unprecedented height of 55 stories. For the newcomer from Missouri, faced with his first skyscraper, the "Cathedral of Commerce," as its detractors called it, was "fascinating to see and to draw." At the same time, however, it brought back a question that had plagued him since student days: "Is there anything really Gothic about an American office building?" And it aroused the desire to strike out on less familiar paths. With his employer's encouragement, he located a small studio in midtown Manhattan, and in 1915, after three years in Gilbert's office, he was on his own as an architectural delineator.[21]

His first free-lance drawings were lively pen-and-ink studies of the streets and buildings of Greenwich Village, where he and his wife, Dor-

A Change in Style: Wanamaker's Bridge, 1917.

othy Lapham, herself a successful magazine illustrator, occupied a one-room studio apartment after their marriage in 1914. One early published effort, drawn jointly by "D. and H. Ferriss," appeared in the August 1915 issue of *Vanity Fair*: a page of sketches celebrating "The *Vie de Bohême* in Washington Square."

By 1917, Ferriss's first impressions of the city were replaced by more solid renderings of line and mass. As an illustrator of wartime subjects for the federal government's Committee on Public Information,[22] his bold studies of behind-the-scenes activities at army bases, shipyards and munition plants appeared as propaganda for Liberty Loan drives and as full-page news pictures in the New York *World* and *Tribune* and in *The Christian Science Monitor.* On-the-spot sketches were also published that vividly recall the ebullient mood of patriotism that swept this country during the First World War.

With these wartime industrial drawings, Hugh Ferriss began to come into his own. In August 1918, the *Architectural Review* of Boston was the first to present his studies of "huge structural masses" as a novel and refreshing change from the pen-and-ink studies of European travel scenes and classical details that hitherto had filled the pages of American journals of architecture. In describing Ferriss's technique, the article noted that unlike many contemporary draftsmen he never worked over a pencil outline laid out by another hand and that he always had in mind the total effect desired even before he began to draw. The first stage of each rendering was a rough sketch—about half a dozen lines—that later was worked into final form in his studio, while he still retained a strong mental image of the structure, but was no longer distracted by details. The finished product was the result of constant experiment with various materials: charcoal and carbon pencil and lithographic crayon applied so thickly that highlights could be scraped out with razor or knife and edges blurred, with gloved finger or paper stump, to produce a rough, smudged effect. Kneaded erasers were used to produce highlights and modeling, while pastels supplied traces of turquoise and terracotta, ochre and brown. An assortment of drawing papers was employed as well, some textured, others highly glazed.[23]

Sub-Treasury Building, Wall Street. From "New York in Wartime," *Vanity Fair*, October 1918.

Setbacks:
"The New Architecture"

O F ALL THE men whom he knew and worked with in the 1920s—and their names read now like a *Who Was Who* of American architecture—the most influential in the launching of Ferriss's own career was Harvey Wiley Corbett, one of this country's most articulate promoters of the burgeoning skyscraper. Corbett's light touch in selling tall buildings to his clients was observed by Ferriss on his first visit to the architect's office, then located on the top floor of the newly completed Bush Terminal Building on West 42nd Street. As the artist entered the spacious drafting room, he found Corbett—"a tall figure silhouetted against a bird's-eye view of Times Square"—intently contemplating what appeared to be a neatly constructed scale model of a 20-story building. This object, however, turned out to be a box which, as Corbett pulled a hidden string, released a second building concealed inside the first. Inside the second,

however, was a third, and the clients, impressed by the theatricality of the event, finally built a building considerably higher than the one originally intended.[24]

For both men, this encounter marked the start of a new phase in their work. For Corbett, the Ferriss knack for rendering buildings yet unbuilt proved a means of republicizing in dramatic visual terms a wide variety of plans, ranging from a scheme for elevated sidewalks in midtown Manhattan[25] to a proposed replica of King Solomon's Temple.[26] For Ferriss, Corbett's firm grasp of structural principles gave ballast to his own more fanciful schemes, while the older man's affinity for new ideas made him a congenial friend and teacher.

Perhaps their most absorbing topic of conversation was the recently enacted New York zoning law of 1916—the first of its kind in the nation—which, at the time of their first meeting, had not yet begun to take effect in actual buildings. Before passage of this pioneering law, there was nothing to prevent skyscrapers from rising straight up on their lot lines like so many gigantic boxes, thus cutting off light and air from less fortunate neighbors and drastically reducing property values in adjacent areas. The 37-story Equitable Building of 1915 was a notorious case in point.[27] To end this chaotic state of affairs, the new regulations attacked the skyscraper on three fronts: by dividing the city into building zones defined by commercial or residential use; by mandating varying areas of open space within these zones; and, finally, by requiring that tall buildings be set back from the street in order to admit more light and air into the streets. It was the last ordinance, governing the height of buildings, that was of the most direct concern to New York architects.[28]

As Corbett and Ferriss were quick to observe, the drafters of the law were guided by purely practical considerations. Little, if any, thought had been given to the effect of the setback provision on the actual design of buildings. Corbett's immediate response to the challenge was to prepare a series of diagrams defining the exact parameters of the prescribed building envelope. Using the Corbett diagrams as a guide, Ferriss then set about composing a series of perspective drawings that depicted, in the most concrete possible terms, the gradual evolution of city buildings under the zoning law. These drawings were first published in *The New York Times* of March 19, 1922, as illustrations for an article on "The New Architecture," in which the artist predicted a revolution in architectural design. Taken together, they were a step-by-step guide to construction of the ideal setback skyscraper of the future.

To the designer's eye, the most striking single result of the new law was the pyramidal form that it implied, a rough-hewn bulk that he likened to a mass of clay awaiting the sculptor's hand. He foresaw whole cities of pyramids, whose "superimposed, receding stages" would present a panorama as inspiring as that of the great monuments of ancient Egypt. Where the cubelike buildings of the pre-law period were typically finished only on the side facing the street, the new pyramids would force architects to become sculptors of entire buildings, rather than mere decorators of facades. In place of box-like behemoths, casting their gloomy shadows on the street below, the new setbacks would rise into the sun, with hanging gardens abloom on their ledges: "To reach the out-of-doors," the artist wrote, "New Yorkers will not go away; they will go up."

In Ferriss's view the New York zoning law implied nothing less than "the new architecture of a civilization."[29] Although his estimates of its exact time of arrival were somewhat elastic, ranging from a generation or so to half a century, he had no doubt that large areas of the contemporary city eventually would be razed to make way for the coming metropolis.[30]

F OR FERRISS, the zoning law marked the start of his rise to success. Writing to his father, Franklin Ferriss, in the fall of 1923, the artist expressed hope of a wider scope for his work: "Between ourselves, I very little value my abilities as a delineator. . . . I must either prove myself a creator, dealing with structural masses, or admit that my career is negligible. . . . If I had the time to give to it, I should be able to make an exhibition-full of original drawings of interest to all who are concerned with the present and future of New York (and) be able to predict and study these future forms in my drawings even more effectively than a practicing architect, who is necessarily occupied for a long time on each building he undertakes."

During the following months, despite an increasingly active practice, Ferriss devoted his spare time to visualizations of the metropolis that, he believed, would result from progressive architectural trends just getting underway. By April of 1925, a group of 27 "Drawings of the Future City" were ready for display in the first one-man exhibit of the artist's work at the Anderson Galleries, then located at 59th Street and Park Avenue.[31] A number of these futuristic renderings, photographically enlarged to mural size and painted over by the artist, were included a few months later in a large "Tercentenary Pictorial Pageant of New York" at the John Wanamaker department store in downtown Manhattan.[32] With these drawings the impact of Ferriss's work on contemporary architectural design became an acknowledged fact. The Shelton Hotel and the American Radiator Building, both early results of the setback law, were

"The Metropolis of Tomorrow"

23

already complete, and they bore a remarkably close resemblance to Ferriss's drawings. *Vanity Fair* pronounced the artist "a force in the creation of our American architecture," who "inspired many of our architects to realize his dreams in steel and stone." Architect John Mead Howells wrote: "You are certainly helping to form the 'American style' that the newspapers call for so loudly and helping the rest of us to follow you." In 1925, an assessment of the artist's work appeared in *American Art News:* "There was a great deal of heated opposition to the zoning law in New York, but Mr. Ferriss showed the architects that the new restriction was in reality a splendid possibility. . . . His drawings of buildings are one of the few expressions of the modern spirit which leave one with the feeling that it may be possible for our age actually to contribute something of its own."[33]

To close followers of Ferriss's work, the publication four years later of his *Metropolis of Tomorrow* came as no surprise. The book was in large part a compilation of his best-known drawings of the previous decade.[34] Following the arrangement of pictures in his first exhibition of 1925, the artist divided the illustrations into three groups, which moved from a straightforward record of contemporary realities to original designs for the future. In the first, "Cities of Today," the artist pictured 17 skyscrapers that he regarded as significant results of the zoning law. They ranged in location from New York to Los Angeles and in time from Bertram Goodhue's proposed "Convocation Tower" of c. 1921 (page 81) to the Empire State, the latter then in the earliest stages of construction and still known as the Waldorf-Astoria Office Building from its location on the site of the old Waldorf-Astoria Hotel.

From existing structures the author turned in "Projected Trends" to an assessment of the city that, he thought, would come into being if various architectural tendencies then underway should continue unchecked. On the debit side, Ferriss caricatured continuing trends toward evergreater building heights and ever-growing congestion in traffic, conjuring up fearful visions of vast towers of the future, their rooftops joined by stacked rows of ramps for automobiles (page 44).[35] On the credit side, he portrayed a number of progressive proposals for future development: the setback skyscraper and the multiblock building, raised sidewalks for pedestrians, and the growing use of improved construction materials. In one drawing, first displayed in New York's Machine-Age Exposition of 1927, the artist pictured a city made entirely of glass (pages 56–57).

In the last pages of his book the artist unveiled his "Imaginary Metropolis," a designer's dream in which the "stupid and miscellaneous" environment of contemporary New York would be replaced by a firmly structured arrangement of "viewpoint and vista, axis, relation and plan."[36] Instead of the "close juxtaposition of formidable masses" that characterized the existing city, the artist proposed widely spaced structures of even more formidable proportions, the tallest of them rising a thousand feet from the sidewalk (about the height of the completed Empire State) and equivalent in bulk to six or eight city blocks. Three of these huge complexes were to be set in triangular formation at the heart of Ferriss's city, each dominating one of three principal zones of human endeavor (for science, business, and art) and each surrounded by lower buildings that radiated fanwise in decreasing order of height to the outlying residential

Progressive Views of a Rendering. From Ferriss article on architectural rendering that appeared in *Encyclopaedia Britannica* from 1929 to 1961.

districts of that city. The general effect would be that of "a wide plain . . . from which rise, at considerable intervals, towering mountain peaks."

The exact nature of these intervals was the result of numerous studies made by the artist in preceding years, in which he explored the appearance of buildings set various distances apart from one another. In *Metropolis* he recommended a minimum space of half a mile between major skyscrapers. Despite its novel appearance this arrangement of space and mass was a logical extension of current laws regulating the height and volume of buildings.[37]

The handling of metropolitan traffic was, for Ferriss, "the problem of problems." The largest skyscrapers of his proposed city were also traffic stations, to be located at the connecting points of 200-foot wide expressways. An elaborate system of off-street parking was envisaged for the business district, with high-speed traffic relegated to levels below the street. Perhaps the most controversial aspect of Ferriss's imaginary metropolis was his handling of pedestrian traffic. By 1929, Corbett's relatively modest proposal for raised sidewalks in midtown Manhattan had developed, under the artist's pencil, into a citywide system of pedestrian plans elevated a story or two above street level, a theme that also formed the subject matter of some of his later drawings.[38] During the early 1930s, Ferriss had in mind as a sequel to *Metropolis* a book of designs for a city plan based on a complete separation of vehicular and pedestrian traffic. A number of illustrations for this proposal appeared in a 1932 exhibition of the artist's work at the Roerich Museum in New York, but the book itself fell victim to the Depression and was never published.[39]

It was only in his visualizations of future passenger travel by air, then still in the earliest stages of commercial development in the United States, that Ferriss departed from contemporary models to project ideas that now appear closer to science fiction than to fact. Airports were to be located within "a mile or so" of the business center, with landing "shelves" for airplanes conveniently placed atop the tallest skyscrapers.[40] In one 1930 drawing (pages 72–73), the artist even fancied an airport terminal shaped like a gigantic stalagmite, a form suggested by the "Mooring Mast" for dirigibles then under construction on the summit of the Empire State.

In the flurry of words that greeted his proposals for the future, few observers noted that visualizations by Ferriss were based on a stern indictment of the existing city nor that it was his very disenchantment with the present that prompted his dream of better things to come.[41] For city planners with a regional bias these "theatrical and moonstruck" sketches—as Lewis Mumford called them—merely projected all the least desirable features of contemporary New York.[42] For confirmed city-dwellers, by contrast, *The Metropolis of Tomorrow* appeared as nothing short of utopia. However, no matter what their opinion of his ideas, the critics were in general agreement that Ferriss's work had made a sizable dent on the architectural thinking of the '20s.

THE IMPACT of the New York zoning law could not be ignored. By 1929 it had spread, with various local modifications, to over 300 cities[43] and in the words of G. H. Edgell, dean of Harvard's School of Architecture, had become "the most interesting single phenomenon in American architecture today."[44] Seen purely from the standpoint of design, however, it was clear that zoning had not even begun to create the new era of architecture predicted by Ferriss seven years before. The handsome pyramids recorded in his drawings were greatly outnumbered by ziggurat-like affairs that he called "wedding cakes," shaped by their builders to enclose the maximum amount of rentable space, while still conforming to the letter of the law. As Lewis Mumford put it: "The setback skyscraper is rapidly turning out to be the great booby-prize in American architecture, and by now it has become pretty plain that building ordinances and ideal schemes by Mr. Hugh Ferriss cannot take the place of a genuine aesthetic command over the materials, structure and site."[45]

The picture, however, was not all dark. Even as the Depression fell, bringing construction to a stop throughout the country, Ferriss noted "a certain starkness and even nakedness" that was, he wrote in the fall of 1929, "becoming the norm for all newly-arisen forms."[46] A new austerity in design had already been seen in the Daily News Building (pages 88–89) and soon would be evident in the Philadelphia Savings Fund Society Building of 1932 (page 90). By 1933, the new slimmed-down silhouette had found its apogee in the "Slab," a nickname first applied to the RCA Building at Rockefeller Center and later to a host of imitators throughout the country.

Writing for the *New Yorker* that December, Lewis Mumford was the first to note a resemblance between what he then regarded as the "grandiose inanities" of "Mr. Rockefeller's Center" and buildings envisaged by Ferriss several years before.[47] In fact, Ferriss's contribution to the project was limited to renderings of the first and final stages of de-

"Power in Buildings"

Bush House, London, Corbett & Helmle, Architects. From Ferriss article, "Three Stages of a Rendering," *Pencil Points*, January 1921.

sign, although its final form embodied a number of progressive design trends illustrated by Ferriss in earlier drawings (pages 92–93). Today, Rockefeller Center still stands as a turning point in urban design—a summing up of the best architectural thinking of the previous decade and a promise of plans yet to be realized elsewhere in this country.

During the 1930s Ferriss, like others in his field, made do with whatever projects came his way. Almost overnight, it seemed, the towers of his imaginary metropolis of the future paled and then vanished altogether before the grim reality of the Great Depression. When urban building resumed once more, the artist's work, like the buildings he portrayed, had undergone a transformation; new ideas were in the air; prophecies were out of style; illustrations of real, not imaginary, structures were in demand. In a 1940 assessment of the Roosevelt years, Ferriss publicly proclaimed that "the era of banks and skyscrapers is at an end"—a not-unreasonable conclusion considering that with the sole exception of Rockefeller Center, the United States, during the previous decade, had produced no major skyscrapers. In their place were structures of a different kind: the massive power plants and factories, airports and highways that, to the artist's eye, constituted both the most arresting and the most ominous architecture of the day. Although Pearl Harbor was still to come, it was impossible to escape the conclusion, as Ferriss later wrote, that "war already was being waged in buildings."[48]

In the summer of 1941, subsidized by a grant from The Architectural League of New York, Ferriss set out on a six-month tour of the country to record his choice of the best in new American buildings.[19] Many of his subjects were better known to the public by form and function than by the names of their builders. Others, however, were far from anonymous: a steel foundry designed by Albert Kahn of Detroit (pages 120–121); Eliel Saarinen's Academy of Art in Cranbrook, Michigan; the Johnson Wax Building in Racine, Wisconsin, by Frank Lloyd Wright (pages 114–116).

By the time Ferriss returned to New York in 1942, 18,000 miles and 40 states later, he had completed a sizable collection of drawings and sketches to illustrate the more impressive structures seen on his journey. The best of these were exhibited at The Architectural League and were later included in a one-man show of the artist's work at the Whitney Museum of American Art. A number of drawings from the series subsequently appeared in an "American Industry at War" exhibit at the Metropolitan Museum of Art and eventually formed the nucleus of *Power in Buildings*. In the spring of 1943, the artist became one of ten recipients of grants awarded that year by the American Academy and Institute of Arts and Letters. In the citation that accompanied his award, Ferriss was commended for drawings of "pure geometric form on a grand scale."[50]

Teamwork:
The United Nations
Headquarters

BY THE MID-1940s, having survived a crushing economic setback and a Second World War, American architects were once again able to plan for the future, and Ferriss's work became, as before, a reflection of the national urge to build. His drawings of that period covered a broad spectrum of design, ranging from the wartime bomb shelter proposed for installation below the Palisades (pages 128–129) to a peacetime remodeling of the Metropolitan Museum of Art, the subject of one of his most Piranesi-like drawings (page 125). In 1945, the artist visualized proposed additions for New York's major airport and for half a dozen large manufacturing plants, among them a stylish new Technical Center for General Motors in Detroit (page 117).

Although his relationship with practicing architects had been, until then, on a one-to-one basis, Ferriss now found himself employed as consultant to numerous large boards of design that began to proliferate at about this time in response to the increasing complexity and sophistication of urban building. His work as a design consultant for the New York World's Fair of 1939 (pages 112–113) was an early case in point. Of all the major teamwork projects with which he was involved, however, the most demanding was the complex problem in design presented by the proposed United Nations Headquarters in New York in the late 1940s (pages 96–97).

The story of Ferriss's involvement with this challenging assignment began on a curious note. In March of 1946, he joined an ad hoc board of architects and engineers appointed by the then-mayor of New York William O'Dwyer to explore the potential of Flushing Meadows on Long Island as a permanent home for the United Nations. The artist was well acquainted with the former World's Fair site, and his work proceeded smoothly. Final drawings of the UN proposal, as submitted to the General Assembly, conveyed a bucolic impression of low buildings surrounded by trees on 350 acres of landscaped grounds.[51]

Later that summer, while the assembly delegates were still in session at Flushing Meadows, Ferriss was commissioned by the architectural firm of Harrison and Abramovitz to visualize a $25 million housing development in midtown Manhattan, proposed by real-estate tycoon William Zeckendorf for a site between First Avenue and the East River, bounded by 42nd and 48th Streets.[52]

Only a few weeks later, the New York papers broke the news that for a mere $8.5 million, John D. Rockefeller, Jr. had purchased the site of "X-City" and had offered to donate it to the United Nations.[53] Within hours of reading the banner headlines, Ferriss—after hasty consultations by phone with various officials and architects involved in the project—completed a drawing designed to show how 17½ acres of a cramped Manhattan slum could be transformed into an airy and spacious home for the United Nations. The result of his charette was before the assembly delegates first thing the next morning when they met to consider the Rockefeller offer[54] and may well have influenced their decision to accept it. Shortly after the first meeting of the UN design board, in January 1947, Ferriss moved his drawing materials to Suite 2700 of the RKO Building at Rockefeller Center which, for the following year, served as a combined workshop and office for members of the staff. As architect in charge of the presentation drawings and perspective design studies, he prepared renderings for use in progress reports to the press and to the UN itself. Ferriss also functioned as a simultaneous translator, recording and reconciling countless, often conflicting, proposals put forward by the ten distinguished members of the international design team, focusing their attention on basic mass and structural relationships and patiently noting the advantages and shortcomings of the various plans under discussion.[55]

DURING THE last two decades of his career Ferriss served as a member of various groups concerned with city architecture, among them the New York City Art Commission and the Municipal Art Society. As president of both The Architectural League of New York and the New York chapter of the American Institute of Architects, his ability to soothe and reconcile opposing groups within his profession was proverbial. One of the most successful exhibitions that he staged at the League in the late 1930s and early 1940s was devoted to a comprehensive display of work by well-known architectural adversaries, which he called *Versus*.[56]

Ferriss's middle-of-the-road position in later years grew out of a radical reassessment of his earlier role as an architectural visionary. Within the context of the '20s, he had been in the forefront of the new architecture, allying himself squarely with those designers who, despite a solid Beaux-Arts background, were willing to take the consequences of new structural demands and to allow each project, as Ferriss wrote in 1923, to "evolve its own outward forms from its own native elements."[57] However, like many of his more progressive colleagues, the artist was by no means ready to abandon the traditions in which he had been schooled. The sphinxes and winged horses that so often appeared as grace notes in his drawings were tributes to the order and elegance that, he believed, should characterize the architecture of any age, past or present. In a radio broadcast of 1930—a dialogue with Frank Lloyd Wright on the subject of "This Modern Architecture"—Ferriss argued that architecture, however "modern," was always firmly rooted in the past, and Wright replied: "I think Mr. Ferriss has established an important fact. The "New" architects are "New" merely because they are more true to tradition, almost, than tradition can be true to itself. The New is ever Old and the Old is ever New."[58]

By the end of the '20s, the designer's name was frequently bracketed with that of Le Corbusier, whose 1929 book, *The City of Tomorrow*, appeared simultaneously with Ferriss's *Metropolis*. During the next few years, however, it became increasingly clear that despite a certain visual likeness between ideas they put forward a decade before, the difference in outlook between the two men could scarcely have been more extreme.[59] To Le Corbusier on his first trip to New York in 1935, the effects of the zoning law—by then fully apparent—appeared "deplorably romantic," while the towering setbacks regarded by most Americans as the last word in architectural sophistication were branded as "naive, touching, idiotic" and much too small, besides.[60] To Ferriss, the pronouncements of the new functionalists seemed as dogmatic in their way as those of an earlier generation of eclectics that he himself had rejected.

By 1953 in *Power in Buildings*, the artist's parochial enthusiasm of an earlier era had been replaced by a lofty air of detachment. His florid prose, so typical of the '20s, had given way to a low-keyed, almost conversational style, and his one-time visions of the future city were conspicuous by their absence. Of 60 illustrations, only a handful portrayed the soaring skyscrapers that had once claimed his undivided attention. So solidly based were the massive forms favored by Ferriss in his later drawings that to some observers (judging by the severe design standards of the early '50s), they implied an outright rejection on the artist's part of the lean and airy shapes of modern architecture. A *New York Times* review of *Power in Buildings* by the writer and editor, Peter Blake, reflects this view: "Ferriss . . . is so greatly interested in 'powerful' architecture that if he tried to sketch a birdhouse it would end up looking like Boulder Dam. Now, the trouble is, of course, that most modern architecture, of the post-war vintage at least, is not like that. With very few exceptions, architects are working toward a concept of glassier, sparer structures that reflect the vastly increased strength of our materials and the vastly increased skill of our engineers. . . . The most convincing drawings in this book are those showing masonry or concrete structures. Ferriss speaks (and writes) softly, but he carries an awfully big pencil. Still, there is little question that he is the most impressive artist in this particular game."[61]

As a philosopher of his profession, Ferriss was much in demand as a public speaker, his popularity arising not so much because he pro-

A Vision of the Great Porch at Night, replica of "Solomon's Temple" by Corbett & Helmle, Architects. From *Pencil Points*, November 1925.

pounded new or startling ideas but because he put in perspective the basic architectural issues of the day. Throughout the contentious period that followed the Depression, he remained aloof from the divisive wrangling that by then had split American architects into rival camps: on one side, the Beaux-Arts-trained traditionalists, still clinging to the past; on the other, disciples of the styleless new international style. Time and again he returned to his central theme: the need to heal the rift that had occurred in his lifetime between the art and the science of architecture.

As Ferriss saw it, the division between architect and engineer that he had first observed as a student, shortly after the turn of the century, had steadily widened and deepened as the country's leading architects, despite vast gains in method and materials, continued to employ styles borrowed from the past, while during the 1930s, by way of contrast, the rise of a new technology had threatened to submerge the art of architecture altogether. The result of this dichotomy, Ferriss argues, was a "civil war," in which "physical function was opposed to psychological function, scientist to artist, modern to traditional." The traditionalist produced "beautiful facades that no longer worked"; the modernist, "workable packages devoid of beauty." It was the lack of synthesis between these two opposing viewpoints that in large part accounted for the limitations of architectural design in his lifetime.

The profound, if often unrealized, effect of the design of buildings on their inhabitants was a basic motif of *The Metropolis of Tomorrow*. Twenty-five years later Ferriss was still pointing the way to architecture's uniquely constructive goal: "Others may teach or preach synthesis in man's life; architects can build it into his surroundings, and through the massive influence of environment can directly affect his life."[62]

TODAY, Hugh Ferriss's work has surfaced on a wave of nostalgia for the American past, and it is widely conceded as a major factor in the consciousness-raising of his colleagues toward acceptance of new forms in architectural design. It was his special gift to observe new trends and proposals and translate them into a coherent picture of the future. Taking his cue from plans still on the drawing board, Ferriss was one of the first designers in this country to realize, through his drawings, the design potential of the steel frame skyscraper. Although he laid no claims to prophetic vision, his metropolis has in numerous respects withstood the test of time. The "cloud-capped towers of a vision"[63] that appeared as mere dreams in drawings of half a century ago are commonplace realities today, as are the curtain walls of shaped and colored glass that the artist saw then only in his mind's eye.

However, it must be conceded that the megalopolis sketched by Hugh Ferriss and defined by like-minded architects of fifty years ago has proven more valid in detail than in its grand design.[64]

It is a measure of the enduring relevance of Ferriss's work that he remained so deeply immersed in the day-to-day evolution of the city throughout a period that embraced profound changes in both the theory and the practice of architecture. Today, there are heartening signs that the reunion of the art and science of architecture heralded by Ferriss is at hand.

Like many another blueprint for the future, the "metropolis of tomorrow" has fallen short of expectation, but the buildings that Hugh Ferriss drew stand today as prototypes of the modern skyscraper: for the architect, a call to better design; for the draftsman, a reminder of standards yet to be equalled.

A Contribution to the Profession

HUGH FERRISS:

By Paul Goldberger

A HALF-CENTURY has passed since the publication of Hugh Ferriss's most significant work, *The Metropolis of Tomorrow* in 1929, and since many of Ferriss's important drawings were executed. The drawings themselves, and the books within which they were collected, are documents of a remarkable era in American architecture and planning, a time in which the American contribution to urban architecture—the skyscraper—was manifesting itself across the land in greater and greater quantities, greater and greater size, and greater and greater variety.

Ferriss was a prophet of the new skyscraper and of the new city. It is hard to know whether to call him artist, architect, city planner, visionary designer, or urban philosopher: he was a part of all these things. He drew the skyscraper designs of other architects with such eloquence that his renderings have become the standard visual representation of many buildings. But more important than Ferriss's work in service of other architects' schemes was his use of his pen to reveal his own visions of what the city might be. More than any other American artist or planner of his time, Hugh Ferriss foresaw the great impact the skyscraper would have on the American city and sought to give the highrise city coherent and civilized form. His visions of the new city preceded those of Norman Bel Geddes or Raymond Hood; they can be said to have played a part in shaping these influential schemes for new, technologically oriented urban centers.

Ferriss was a curious combination of the romantic and the realist: he emerges directly out of that tradition of romantic pragmatism that yielded such architects as James Gamble Rogers, Bertram Goodhue, Daniel Burnham, John Russell Pope, and Cass Gilbert, an attitude that merged a theatrical, almost fanciful view of architectural form with a strongly practical sense of economics, technology, and planning. Ferriss was far less inclined to accept the direct reuse of historical form than these architects generally were, but he was even more romantic than they in his view of what the city might become.

His works would be crucial objects to us today if only for their beauty, which is so striking as to make even a confirmed antiurbanist rethink his convictions. But they are more important still as early achievements in the quest toward eloquent shape for the gargantuan skyscraper form—a quest that seems to have renewed energy today as architects are again possessed by the urge to sculpt the skyscraper, to find alternatives to the Miesian box that has become the postwar vernacular. As architects from Philip Johnson to Cesar Pelli, from Hugh Stubbins to I. M. Pei seem determined to design forms of varied massing, with unusual skins and often elaborate tops, Ferriss's drawings seem once again a relevant model.

But Ferriss's work is perhaps most urgent right now for the message that underlay all his urban design schemes: his perceptions of the dangers of unplanned, unguided growth of skyscrapers. The construction booms of the 1960s and late 1970s have led to a period of such intense concentration in the core of major cities as to be considered a serious crisis. It is a situation which Ferriss foresaw and tried, with all the resources available to an artist, architect, and writer, to prevent.

In *The Metropolis of Tomorrow*, Ferriss wrote with deep concern that "The most popular image of the Future City—to judge by what is most often expected from the draftsman's pencil—is composed of buildings which, without any modification of their existing nature, have simply grown higher and higher. . . . A 60-story tower in New York evokes a 70-story tower in Chicago. What is more serious, a 60-story tower in New York evokes a 70-story tower directly across the street. The skyscraper is said to be America's premier architectural contribution to date; popular fancy pictures the future contribution to be rows of still higher skyscrapers; in other words, it pictures 70-story skyscrapers side by side for miles. . . . do we not begin to apprehend, in this headlong ascent, something ominous?"

To accompany these paragraphs he offered a drawing entitled "Crowding Towers" (page 45), an imaginary view of block after block of high towers squeezing tightly against each other, forcing out space for sun and air and traffic. The drawing has Ferriss's characteristics—a solemn yet oddly lilting air to it, as if the heavy towers were lit by a mysterious light, and it shows towers of masonry, not of glass, but otherwise it looks remarkably like much of midtown Manhattan right now. If anything, Ferriss's vision is too restrained: Manhattan in the east 50s is already built up far beyond the degree Ferriss illustrates, a degree which he calls a "serious menace."

Ferriss was quite level-headed about the alternatives. He rejected Frank Lloyd Wright's view that cities should be dispersed and skyscrapers built only in the countryside: "The opinion is frequently and forcefully expressed, by sincere critics, that our sole hope lies . . . in decentralization. But . . . this must be dismissed as a mere dream. For the imagination, it paints a lovely picture—just as a memory of Colonial towns is lovely, but in all that is actually going on about us, there is nothing to be seen which gives the slightest substance to it. . . . call it what you will: gregarious instinct or economic necessity: the primary trend, with which we must deal in any formulation of the future city, is the trend toward centralization."

FERRISS SAW his mission, then, as guiding this dense, centralized city toward a sensible shape. He offered many partial schemes and one total plan for the city that is worthy of attention, if hardly of adoption. Ferriss's imaginary city plan called for a metropolis of major centers for commerce, for art, and for science and technology, each a complex of great towers surrounded by lower buildings. The centers would be set far apart from each other, on an overall plan of great formal, radial avenues reminiscent of the plans of Daniel

Toward an Ideal City

Burnham, and each center would have an architectural identity to suggest its function. The business center's buildings are to be soaring, elegantly massed towers of masonry suggestive of Schultze & Weaver's design for the Waldorf-Astoria Hotel on Park Avenue in New York. The art center's towers are lighter, luminous almost, with roof gardens and sun terraces; the science and technology center is housed in a sharply defined, Art Moderne structure whose lines resemble that of a streamlined locomotive.

This city is based on a number of fallacious notions; it is not difficult to observe that it requires an almost socialistic kind of government to guarantee smooth relationships between the various centers, and when Ferriss's additional schemes for a single tower to house all religions and for a center of philosophy at the intersection of the art and science zones of the city are considered, the plan seems not merely impractical but touchingly naive. At this point it seems almost excessive to point out the further shortcomings: that Ferriss envisioned a city frozen in time, with little room to grow and change; that he saw a city with little spontaneity, allowing only for planned elements; and that his plan would have presented innumerable difficulties in terms of governance.

But the "Imaginary Metropolis," as Ferriss termed it, was a polemic. It was an ideal city, to be viewed as part of the tradition of visionary dream cities, its real purpose to awaken us to the failures of real cities—in this case, to the perils of overcrowding; of excessive striving for heights; of inadequate provision for pedestrians, vehicular traffic, and open space; and of inadequate attention to the esthetic demands of the new skyscraper form.

Ferriss is at his best when he is in between dreams and realities—in between expressions of his excessively romantic ideal city and the renderings he created of the real designs of others. His "Crowding Towers" drawing is an example of this: it is at once an earnest vision and a piece of common sense. Similar, if less prescient, were several schemes for placement of pedestrian and vehicular traffic on separate levels in the city; although this had been proposed time and time again over the years, beginning long before Ferriss's time, his versions are clear and thoughtful. [Characteristically, there are two versions—one an extravagant but not really serious suggestion for a highway running along building setbacks 20-stories up, with aerial airplane runways as well (page 44); the other drawing a much more feasible scheme for adding a pedestrian walkway to major streets such as Fifth Avenue one floor above the present street level.]

Equally indicative of Ferriss's balance between romantic ideals and pragmatic concepts is his scheme for a combination church and office building. The drawing, entitled "Churches Aloft" (not included in this book), was prompted by Ferriss's realization that the skyscrapers had robbed the church spire of its traditional dominative role in the skyline. "With skyscrapers towering above the spire of the average church, and with land values also mounting beyond its income, what is that church to do? Move away from the very arena whose activities it is, avowedly to influence?" Ferriss wrote. He observed with disapproval the few efforts which had been made to join churches to commercial property by placing a church in the vaguely Gothicized base of an otherwise ordinary apartment house or office tower. He then went on to offer a logical and elegantly simple alternative: a church on top of a tower, as the crown of a skyscraper.

Ferriss's proposal seemed especially relevant in the mid-1970s as Citicorp Center, the multiuse complex sponsored by Citibank in New York, came into being, with a 900-foot bank headquarters looming over the new St. Peter's Lutheran Church. The architect may well have accurately rendered unto Caesar that which was Caesar's here, but the symbolism is disconcerting to say the least: it is the bank that lifts its head up high, the church that nestles low. One can hardly conceive of Ferriss's scheme being accepted as a logical alternative by the bank, but it would surely have solved the symbolism problem. Ferriss believed that God ranked over Mammon, and more important, he saw a logical and rational way in which architecture might make this hierarchy clear, and hence bring a sense of order to the entire city.

Order is perhaps too important to Ferriss: his zeal for it is surely what compromises his idealized city, and the search for it remains a theme throughout all his works. Chaos is bad, order is good, we are told by both his words and his pictures. He begins *The Metropolis of Tomorrow* with the shocked observation that the city of New York "is not designed at all!" and proceeds to denounce the confusion of the existing city in terms severe indeed to us today: "Going down into the streets of a modern city must seem—to the newcomer, at least—a little like Dante's descent into Hades. Certainly so unacclimated a visitor would find, in the dense atmosphere, in the kaleidoscopic sights, the confused noise and the complex physical contacts, something very reminiscent of the lower realms."

These attitudes, more than anything visual in Ferriss's work, date him. For all the concern about overbuilding and excessive densities being expressed today, there is a far greater respect now for heterogeneity in the city than there was in Ferriss's time. Generations raised on the urban theories of Jane Jacobs, Robert Venturi, and Denise Scott Brown tend toward more tolerance of the eccentricities of the urban environment and, scarred as they are by the massively destructive urban renewal efforts of the 1950s and 1960s, toward a distrust of any environment that claims to be a totally planned one. That Ferriss could be so firm in his conviction that there was such a thing as an ideal city at all is, then, more significant than the actual form his idealistic city took; today the very notion of creating an ideal city of any physical shape seems like an effort to improve a false order over natural complexity, an effort that is at best quaint and at worst dangerous.

FERRISS'S MOST famous work remains an early project, the series of drawings done to illustrate the effects of the 1916 New York City zoning ordinances on the forming of future skyscrapers. They were published in 1922 in *The New York Times*, and can be said to have effectively launched Ferriss's career as an urban seer. Before the Ferriss studies, there was considerable uncertainty as to the implications of the 1916 law, which controlled the bulk of skyscrapers built up to the sidewalk by limiting their height and mandating setbacks at specific levels above the street. (The law in effect put an end

Zoning Ordinances and the Shaping of Buildings

to huge, boxy buildings—that is, until it was replaced by a new zoning law in 1961 that, ironically, was written to encourage open space by mandating setbacks at street level. The effect was to create huge, boxy buildings.)

Ferriss, at that point a young architect without designs of his own that would be threatened by the new requirements and with a powerful esthetic sense that suggested to him the possibilities of new skyscraper form, was understandably delighted with the new law. He perceived that it called for a fundamentally pyramidal building form, with height concentrated in the middle of building sites, stepping down to lower masses on the street to permit maximum penetration of light and air. The form fit perfectly with Ferriss's own romantic nature of the skyscraper—soaring towers, majestically set on the cityscape, their tops diminishing into a hazy sky. Ferriss compared the new skyscraper with mountains, a metaphor that seems tired today but was fresh and even daring in 1922: these great things *were* mountains, as awesome as Everest.

Ferriss's series attempted to show the "evolution" of the setback building in the architect's mind. It began with the most basic expression of mass—heavy, pyramidal forms. A second drawing brings the mass to a somewhat more refined shape, with light wells cut in and bulk more precisely articulated. The third stage introduces setbacks instead of the slants of pyramidal form, and the fourth stage refines the setbacks into a practical and visually pleasing mass (pages 52–53).

It is the making of masses which preoccupies Ferriss here, and, indeed, it is no injustice to say that this is his greatest concern throughout his career. He writes almost wistfully of the architect's role as one of "modeling," and he talks of the zoning law as providing "crude clay": "There must come architects who, using the technique of sculptors, will model the crude clay into finished forms."

This was a necessary call, even if it has, to us now, the somewhat naive tone of so much of Ferriss's work, for until Ferriss's time the problem of shaping a building for great height had been given relatively little attention. Louis Sullivan tried to create a theory of skyscraper design, but his work and ideas were a generation old by the 1920s, unsuited to the role of the buildings then rising. The "base, shaft, and capital" formula—an analogy to the classical column, by which a skyscraper would have a formal base, a series of undifferentiated middle floors, and an elaborate top—had been as much of a theoretical underpinning as the period had, but it was ill-suited to the problem of setback design.

Ferriss's buildings were sumptuous; he admired buildings which sat on the ground with a solid presence, yet rose into the sky with a gentle grace. The proportions were sure; if they were not ideal in the plans of the architect whose work Ferriss was rendering, his drawings tended to make them so. His own visionary buildings embraced a variety of styles, but they leaned most toward the subtly ornamented, vertically accented setback shaft of the designs of Raymond Hood, an architect whom Ferriss particularly admired. It is no accident that many of Ferriss's imaginary buildings resemble such works of Hood as The American Radiator Co. Building (page 80) and the Daily News Building (pages 88–89) in New York and conversely that Lewis Mumford found in the original design for Rockefeller Center (pages 92–93), a project in which Hood was a major participant, a strong resemblance to Ferriss's visionary schemes.

It is impossible, of course, to document precisely such reverse influences—such cases of life imitating art, as it were. But there can be no question that Ferriss's drawings of make-believe skyscrapers in the 1920s at once caught the impulses of the architects of the period and stimulated them onward. He gave form on paper to ideas that were germinating in many minds simultaneously; his works on paper were the first real skyscrapers of the 1920s, true progenitors of the stone and steel buildings to follow.

Many of the drawings included in this volume were published originally in Hugh Ferriss's second book, *Power in Buildings*, and they differ somewhat in tone from the earlier works. The theme of the drama inherent in large works of engineering and architecture is one that Ferriss had in fact been exploring subtly throughout his career. His shadings, his perspective, his sense of mysterious light created a haunting tone that gave great power—if perhaps excessive romanticism—to the most mundane building he drew. When he turned his attention in *Power in Buildings* to vast dams and bridges, however, the drama was already there, and his style, instead of providing a new element, seemed to be a restatement, if not even an exaggeration, of the obvious. His views of grain elevators, for example, undoubtedly convey the sense of awesome power which these structures possess. But they lack the straightforward, almost deadpan restraint of the works of Charles Sheeler or Louis Lozowick. Ferriss sets his eye low, so that the grain elevators loom large, making them appear even bigger than they truly are—adding a note of almost contrived drama to their real drama.

The technical skill evident here is, of course, beyond question: Ferriss's work throughout his career was extraordinarily graceful. He understood, far better than any renderer or architect of his time, that buildings were presences, and he gave each structure he drew all that this implies—dignity, strength, movement, mystery, power. His buildings soar, rushing upwards with noble grandeur, yet at the same time they all sit firmly on the ground. Not one could match his ability to make every building appear sumptuous; his skyscrapers sit on streets like grand duchesses at the heads of formal tables, in self-assured command of an ordered world.

That world was, obviously, a world that consisted in part of fantasy—Ferriss had dreams for the city that, as we have seen, were not always grounded in the firmest practicality. But there is another side to Ferriss's romanticism, a side more appealing, perhaps, than the zealous order of his ideal city. Ferriss believed deeply that the city was man's noblest creation and that the means existed to make it work. His city, impractical as it was, is based on the real city, on the New York whose towers he saw from his office window and whose streets he walked.

Ferriss was that very special kind of visionary: one whose dreams were grounded firmly in what was there. He did not want to destroy the city; he did not want to start again—he wanted to use the tools given to him and to his time, to shape a more civilized kind of place. His belief in the skyscraper, if again excessively romantic, was hardly farfetched; the skyscraper has come to play every bit as significant a role as Ferriss envisaged, only with little of the humanistic design his studies had encouraged for it. How much more graceful the skyline Ferriss drew than the cities of cut-off boxes we now have!

Ferriss's lesson, then, is one of vision tempered by accommodation to reality. It is a balance that was rare in Hugh Ferriss's own time; it is rarer still in ours, when the city is either condemned as obsolete or romanticized in terms so mawkish as to embarrass even Ferriss. This balance between vision and reality, between fantasy and common sense, is what motivates all of Ferriss's exquisite, haunting drawings—it is what makes them, finally, testaments not merely to the cities of the imagination, but to the greater cities that exist in real places and in real times.

D R E A M S

If one arrives at the studio at dawn, and if it be a day of fog characteristic of early spring, he finds himself, on raising the shades of the south windows, the lone spectator of a nebulous panorama of mist. . . .

Literally, there is nothing to be seen but mist; not a tower has yet been revealed below, and except for the immediate parapet rail (dark and wet as an ocean liner's) there is not a suggestion of either locality or solidity for the coming scene. . . .

Soon, somewhere off in the mist, a single lofty highlight of gold appears; the earliest beam is upon the tip of the Metropolitan Tower. A moment later, a second; the gilded apex of the New York Life Building. And then, in due succession the other architectural principles lift their pinnacles into vision: the Brooklyn skyscraper group, the Municipal Building, the Woolworth. . . .

As mysteriously as though being created, a Metropolis appears.

1 9 2 2 – 1 9 3 2

The captions are in the artist's own words and in this part of the book are taken primarily from his Metropolis of Tomorrow *of 1929, in which many of these drawings also appeared. Sources of other comments by Ferriss are indicated in Notes for the Drawings, together with background information on their subject matter.*

THE LURE OF THE CITY

"The lure of the city" is the romantic way of phrasing it; imagination sketches the rural youth who is ever arising to his dream of "the big city"—the unformulated yet gleaming metropolis. Call it what you will: gregarious instinct or economic necessity: the primary trend, with which we must deal in any formulation of the future city, is the trend toward centralization.

The opinion is frequently and forcefully expressed, by sincere critics, that our sole hope lies, on the contrary, in decentralization. But, if by the term is meant the dispersal of large centers of population, this must be dismissed as a mere dream. For the imagination, it paints a lovely picture—just as a memory of Colonial towns is lovely; but in all that is actually going on about us, there is nothing to be seen which gives the slightest substance to it.

Left:
OVERHEAD TRAFFIC WAYS

To the skyscraping heights of the Future City, the popular fancy usually adds something remarkable in the way of overhead traffic avenues. Scores of drawings have been produced, showing viaducts at the twentieth floor! Indeed, in some sketches, architectural values have been so completely neglected as to show the taller towers connected at their very pinnacles by a network of aerial traffic bridges which would infallibly cast their gloomy shadow permanently on the city beneath.

Following such leads, one might easily imagine, as in the accompanying drawing, that all "set-backs" of buildings have been aligned and made into automobile highways. One could drive at will across the facades of buildings, at the fifth, tenth, fifteenth or twentieth story. Automobiles below one, automobiles above one! A paradise, perhaps, for the automobile manufacturer! But for the office worker—less and less escape from the noise, the rush and the atmosphere of traffic.

Right:
CROWDING TOWERS

The most popular image of the Future City—to judge by what is most often expected from the draughtsman's pencil—is composed of buildings which, without any modification of their existing nature, have simply grown higher and higher. The popular mind apparently is intrigued by height, as such. A 60-story tower in New York evokes a 70-story tower in Chicago. What is more serious, a 60-story tower in New York evokes a 70-story tower directly across the street. . . .

Certainly there are conscientious city-planners who perceive, in the present trend toward closely juxtaposed towers, a serious menace. The trend indubitably exists; and it is therefore proper, perhaps, for the draughtsman to indicate where it will lead if it is unchecked. Such drawings, however, far from being intended as an inspiration, may serve rather as a warning. "It may look like this—if nothing is done about it."

REVERSION TO PAST STYLES

In the minds of many designers the fundamentals of architectural form were conclusively established by the classic Greeks and Romans. To them design is a matter of adapting and rearranging classical forms within the limitations of a given situation.

These architects will probably accept the new "envelopes"—the forms within which the building must be contained—as a further limitation and, being unrelated to any style, as an unfortunate one. . . .

Classic temples will doubtless keep a foothold, however precarious, on the sheer slope of the pyramid.

A PROPOSAL BY HARVEY WILEY CORBETT: ELEVATED SIDEWALKS, 1923

The increasing traffic congestion which follows in the wake of the mounting skyscraper provokes the thought that more than one traffic level, or numerous traffic levels, must indeed be eventually introduced. . . . In the minds of many experts, the only adequate solution lies in the realm of the third dimension—for instance, placing all pedestrians on a separate plane above that of wheel traffic, and laying all rail traffic on a separate plane below.

To introduce such a system onto Fifth Avenue or State Street or Woodward Avenue would, obviously, involve a tremendous expenditure of money. It would involve a complete and novel revision of store fronts—a shop would in fact have two main entrances; one above for the pedestrian customer and one below for the customer in his car. Yet some such innovation, however radical, seems in the long run inevitable.

A PROPOSAL BY RAYMOND HOOD: APARTMENTS ON BRIDGES, 1929

Not only upward, in skyscrapers, does the city appear forced to move, but also outward—over its bridges. At a recent meeting Architect Raymond Hood outlined the plausible possibility of utilizing the framework of bridges for apartments or offices. The idea could, of course, be visualized in various forms—in the accompanying sketch, the suspension type of bridge is assumed; the towers rise up into fifty or sixty story buildings; the serried structure between is suspended—the buildings literally hung—from cables.

At first glance it would appear that such a location for office or residence is unusually desirable as to exposure, light and air. We may naturally assume landing stages, at the bases of the towers, for launch, yacht and hydroplane—whence it would be only a minute by elevator, to one's private door.

Facetious minds have suggested that the placing of apartments in such a fashion would introduce a bizarre—not to say dangerous—element into domestic life! On the other hand, serious minds have claimed that the project is not only structurally sound but possesses unusual advantages, financially.

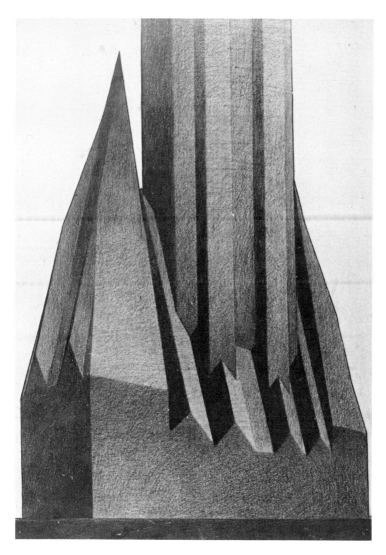

ZONING ENVELOPES, 1922: FIRST STAGE

The writer began to speculate, shortly after the enacting of the law, as to what effects in architectural design were imminent. He discussed the matter with several forward-looking architects, and had the good fortune to find, in the diagrams which Architect Harvey Wiley Corbett was formulating, the practical basis for the first four drawings of the accompanying pictorial study. . . .

The drawing is, briefly, a representation of the maximum mass which, under the Zoning Law, it would be permissible to build over an entire city block. The block is assumed to be two hundred by six hundred feet. The building rises vertically on its lot lines only so far as is allowed by law (in this case, twice the width of adjoining streets). Above this, it slopes inward at specified angles. A tower rises, as is permitted, to an unlimited height, being in area, not over one-fourth the area of the property.

It must be understood that the mass thus delineated is not an architect's design; it is simply a form which results from legal specifications. It is a shape which the Law puts into the architect's hands. He can add nothing to it; but he can vary it in detail as he wishes. It is a crude form which he has to model.

SECOND STAGE

The first step which is taken by the architect is to cut into the mass to admit light into the interior.

It must be borne in mind that the architect is not, in this case, permitting himself any prevision of his final form; there is no pet design toward which he is working. He is accepting, simply, a mass which has been put into his hands; he proposes to modify it, step by step, taking these steps in logical order; he is prepared to view the process impartially and to abide by whatever result is finally reached.

In contemplating the original mass, it was obvious that it contained great interior volumes which were inaccessible to light. He therefore cut out such portions—such "light courts"—as would admit natural light throughout. He finds remaining the form which is shown on the opposite page.

THIRD STAGE

The form as last seen still presented certain peculiarities which, from a practical point of view, are unacceptable. . . . Such decidedly sloping planes as these are alien to accepted notions of construction and demand revision. The architect, therefore, cuts into them again, this time translating them into the rectangular forms which will provide more conventional interior spaces and which can be more economically constructed in steel.

At the same time, he gives consideration to the tower. Legally, it could have risen to any height; as far as engineering limitations are concerned, it could rise considerably higher than any structure now standing. With consideration, however, for the financial aspects of the case—as well as for the other principles which evoked the zoning law—the tower is tentatively limited to one thousand feet.

FOURTH STAGE

Upon contemplating this form, however, it is apparent that yet further revisions will be necessary. The "steps," because of their multitude and their comparatively small dimensions, would not prove an economical venture in steel; clearly, it would be better to remove those steps which do not conform to the usual simple steel grill. Also, the uppermost steps are of too small an area to be of use; when the spaces necessary for elevators and stairs has been set aside, the remaining rentable area would not justify the expense of building.

After removing those parts which were just found to be undesirable, the mass which finally remains is that which is now illustrated. This is not intended, of course, as a finished and habitable building; it still awaits articulation at the hands of the individual designer; but it may be taken as a practical, basic form for large buildings erected under this type of Zoning Law.

BUILDINGS IN THE MODELING

Mention might well be made at this point of the possible effect which the zoned building is having on the professional sculptor. In the Classic and Gothic building, the sculptor was, of course, specifically a collaborator of the architect: each of these styles of architecture evoked its corresponding style of sculptor. And we still find, in such of our modern buildings as are designed in past styles, the appropriate placements for the usual heroic or decorative figures.

But in the great set-backs which are now appearing on our larger buildings, and on their sheer planes, where will those familiar sculptures find a resting place?

It may well be that, ere long, some sculptor will conceive forms which, in scale and spirit, are at one with these new forms of architecture. Or it may be, as is here suggested, that the building in its entirety will be taken to be a sculptor's work.

Right:
THE FINAL MASS CARRIED OUT IN STEEL

Steel will, without doubt, continue to be the structural material for strong buildings for many years to come. It is true that we have been erecting tall structures with it for only a very few decades and we cannot yet claim to be thoroughly familiar with its properties. There are occasional rumors of its permanency being less certain than is yet realized; and there already are suggestions of improved metal substitutes.

In the accompanying study, however, the continued use of steel is taken for granted. Here are also brought together several other . . . contemporary trends . . . the stepping back of buildings along lines of the New York Zoning Law, the utilization of more than one city block as bases for longer structures and ever-increasing altitudes.

GLASS

The new types of glass, which modern ingenuity is already manufacturing, make it quite certain that before long this material will be utilized not simply as windows but as walls.

In steel construction, no specification is implied of the material that must be used for the exterior curtain walls which stand between the steel members; neither brick, stone nor terra cotta is mandatory; any practical material may be considered, and it is already evident that a glass can be produced which is a practical material.

While the thought of a glass building seems to some to be extreme, the material has, in fact, solid advantages. There is an obvious gain in natural light and (with those forms of glass which admit the ultra-violet ray) an increase in the modified rays of the sun. (A possible cooperation appears to be implied between architects and physicians.) The glass need not be visualized as transparent nor as being manufactured in the wide, thin panes now used for windows: in other words, there will not necessarily be the glass houses which invite stones. Glass has, in fact, already been produced in the form of translucent bricks. . . .

It has been suggested that the exterior glass wall may be built of a double thickness (the building thus becoming a sort of thermos bottle); that totally new types of window shades, or screens, may be developed: and that the glass may be made in various colors.

LOFTY TERRACES

The utilization of upper levels, especially in the case of Apartment buildings, has been one of the interesting results of the set-back regulation. Not very long ago, the penthouse on the roof of the building contained only the elevator machinery, the tanks and, occasionally, living quarters for the janitor. The effect of stepping back the building was to draw more attention to the uppermost floor; roof spaces began to be planned on a larger scale as servants' quarters; a few adventurous individuals began to lease some of these floors, throw two or three of the diminutive rooms together and produce apartments which rather surprised their friends. The advantages which were in fact inherent in such locations—increased privacy, exposure, light and air, as well as use of an outdoor space—were increasingly appreciated; architects began to plan them in advance for use as apartments and, in course of time, realtors appreciated the point—that is to say, rents were steeply raised and, at the present moment, the erstwhile janitor's quarters have become the most expensive rentable space in the building.

The use of terraces, fortunately begun, will, without doubt, increase as time goes on, the trend leading to porticoes which will demand a greater share of the architect's attention.

Opposite page:
IMAGINARY METROPOLIS: "BIRD'S-EYE VIEW"

Let us return to the parapet which provided us with our original bird's-eye view of the existing city. It is again dawn, with an early mist completely enveloping the scene. Again, there lies beneath us, curtained by the mist, a Metropolis—and the curtain, again, is about to rise. But, in this case, let us have it rise, not on the existing city, but on a city of the imagination.

As the mists begin to disperse, there come into view, one by one, the summits of what must be quite lofty tower-buildings; in every direction the vistas are marked by these pinnacles as far as the eye can reach. It is apparent that this city, like those with which we had been previously familiar, contains very tall buildings and very many of them; indeed, we may assume, from their dimensions and their disposition over so wide an area, that here is an even greater center of population than anything we had hitherto known.

At the same time, however, we are struck by certain peculiarities in the disposition of the towers now before us. In the first place, no two of them rise in close juxtaposition to each other; roughly calculated, they appear in no case to be less than half-a-mile apart. Also, there is a certain degree of regularity apparent in their disposal throughout; while they are not all precisely equidistant, and their relation does not suggest an absolutely rectangular checkerboard scheme, yet it is obvious that they have been located according to some city-wide plan.

A little later, the general clearing of the scene allows us to check up our first impressions. The tower-buildings rise to a height of a thousand feet from the ground—in a few particular cases, yet higher. And we now see that they spring from very broad bases, as well: their foundations cover three or four city blocks. In the particular cases mentioned, they must cover six or eight blocks.

Yet, in the wide districts which lie between these towers—and which make up by far the greater area of the city—the buildings are all comparatively low. They average six stories; that is to say, they are no higher than the width of the streets which they face. Looking directly down upon the roofs of these buildings, we distinguish a color which suggests the presence of an abundance of planting.

The first confirmed impression of the city is thus of a wide plain, not lacking in vegetation, from which rise, at considerable intervals, towering mountain peaks.

Above:
THE ART CENTER

Presumably there is, in such an architectural landscape, a free access to light and air on the part of all buildings, whether high or low.

A distinct advance has been accomplished in this imaginary city in the matter of smoke elimination: the roofs of all the lower structures have been developed into sun porches and gardens. The fact is, there is two feet of soil on these roofs, and trees are generally cultivated. Open-air swimming pools are frequent.

THE BUSINESS CENTER

Let us scrutinize the streets. The eye is caught by a system of broad avenues which must be two hundred feet wide and which are placed about half a mile apart. One notes that it is precisely at the intersections of these avenues that the tower buildings rise. We may conclude that here is a system of superhighways which carry the express traffic of the city and that the tower buildings are express stations for traffic. . . .

At this closer view we can distinguish in greater detail the characteristics of the tower-buildings. The tower itself rises directly over the intersection of two of the master highways to a height of 1200 feet. There are eight flanking towers, half this height, which, with their connecting wings, enclose four city blocks. The center extends, however, over eight adjoining blocks, where its supplementary parts rise to a height of twelve stories.

Following page:
THE SCIENCE CENTER

Here again is a very high central mass, supported by large wings, the whole extending over adjoining streets to embrace outlying structures. . . .

The traffic plane is wide and calculated to carry a great number of vehicles on more than one level. A waterway is carried down the axis of the main avenue.

PHILOSOPHY

Where art and science meet—that is to say, where
these civic zones contact with one another—there
stands a tower about which are gathered the colleges
of Arts and Sciences.

Since this tower seems to stand somewhat apart, let
us give a moment to examining the particular elements
of its design.

In plan, it seems to show, at all levels, variations of
a nine-pointed star—in other words of three superimposed triangles. Being planned, basically, on the
equilateral triangle, the shaft rises—or, so to speak,
grows—in what seem definite stages. For example, the
vertical dimension from the top of the base up to the
point where the vertical members break for the first
time appears to bear a ratio to the dimension between
this break and the break next above it, as well as to the
total vertical dimension above the latter break. These
three dimensions are to each other as three, one and
three. . . .

The real significance, if any, of a tower having, so to
speak, a threefold plan and a sevenfold ascension, is
obscure. And it is perhaps optimistic to say that here a
number of separate parts aspire to be as one. In any
case, this is the Center of Philosophy.

(a) The Municipal Center

(b) The Vehicular Plane

(c) The Pedestrian Boulevards

PROPOSAL TO SEPARATE PEDESTRIAN FROM VEHICULAR TRAFFIC, 1930

The three studies herewith illustrate a proposal for complete separation between pedestrian and vehicular traffic. The entire ground level of the more congested districts is given over to vehicles (b). . . . In this conception, pedestrian thoroughfares do not take the form of elevated side-walks but of new rights-of-way opened, at second-story level, along center lines of city blocks; these exclusive pedestrian thoroughfares would at first be arcaded through existing buildings; eventually, they would be open boulevards (c). The bird's-eye view (a) shows the vehicular level and the pedestrian thoroughfares in their proposed relationship to each other.

ISOLATED MASSES:
TOWERS OF STEEL AND GLASS

We may safely say that this coming generation will move to abandon the practice,
still current among designers, of evasion
and deception concerning material fact. . . .

Though the public continues, through
habit, to conceive structural strength in
terms of masonry, they will not continue to
misinterpret, for the public's indulgence,
the new language of steel; in a building
where the load is carried more on the interior than the exterior column, they will not
place a facade which states, falsely, that the
greatest load is carried on the corners.

MOORING MAST:
AN AIRPORT OF THE FUTURE

Near a large city, at the intersection of two thoroughfares, there may be four landing fields, a structure containing the "Grand Central Station" and the offices of the airways company—and serving as a mooring mast!

Preceding Page:
IMAGINARY SEAPORT
Left:
SKYSCRAPERS SPANNING STREETS

The underlying proposition is that vertical dimensions of buildings should be in relation to the city's horizontal transportation facilities; more specifically, that skyscrapers should be permitted only where in direct relationship to the rapid transit system. . . .

All tower-buildings are assumed to be express stations of the subway system and to be at least a quarter of a mile apart. A scheme of widely separated towers is held to possess aesthetic as well as practical advantages.

Right:
SKYSCRAPER HANGAR IN A METROPOLIS

The people of New York will practically live in the sky. . . . There will be avenues of aerial gardens and sky golf courses. Instead of going up to the country, the people will go "up" for country air. Towering terraced buildings of the residential zone will give the children a chance to play out of doors. Everybody in the city will spend more time in the open. There will be aerial hangars, and airplanes will be as common as flivvers.

REALITIES

When buildings began to rise, under the New York zoning laws, it was apparent that in most cases we were to have "wedding cakes." These shapes were not the invention or preference of architects, but resulted from the owners' wish to squeeze as much as possible into the envelope, their concern being quantity of rentable space, not quality of design. . . .

But not all buildings were to be "wedding cakes." A search for a sounder form is noticeable in a preliminary study for the Empire State Building made at an early stage of that project, and the achievement of it is seen in the Shelton Hotel [page 84] which, although now hemmed in by miscellaneous structures, continues to stand as a far more simple and impressive form than most of the setback buildings of the subsequent generation. Compare it, however, with Lever House [page 91], which departs from the setback style altogether and announces a different conception of the tall office building.

1 9 2 4   –   1 9 6 8

In this part of the book the captions are taken primarily from Power in Buildings *of 1953, in which many of these drawings also appeared. Sources of other captions are indicated in Notes for the Drawings, together with background information on their subject matter.*

Left:
AMERICAN RADIATOR BUILDING, 1924

40 West 40th Street
Hood & Fouilhoux
The Radiator Building, in New York City, has one undeniable virtue: it has undoubtedly provoked more arguments among laymen on the subject of architectural values than any other structure in the country. . . .

Unhappily, the gold which crowns the tower—and which can be seen gleaming from as far away as Staten Island—cannot be reproduced in this illustration, which pays its respects only to the black. In the black and white rendition one can, indeed, consider the form which . . . is distinctly virile. Yet it is probably the color contrast of the building which gives pause and provokes the valuable discussion. The Radiator building is, in this respect at least, decidedly an experiment. Here is a point to remember when we come to sketch the future city—there are at least a few trained and experienced architects who have no fear of experimentation.

Right:
THE CONVOCATION TOWER

Proposed by Bertram Grosvenor Goodhue
An impressive tower—a beautiful subject for the draughtsman; not to be counted among buildings actually erected—but to be included in this survey because it was one of the last conceptions of a designer who, throughout all his works, greatly influenced the direction of American architecture: the late Bertram Grosvenor Goodhue.

This structure was proposed for a site adjoining Madison Square Garden; as may be guessed from its appearance, it was to house, on the main floor, a great auditorium (in fact, a church) and above this, the huge shaft containing offices was to rise some thousand feet from the ground.

There are critics who will say that it seems of stone rather than of steel, and they may not add that the buttressed corners (which contain elevator shafts and stairways) were designed in disregard of the financial value of corner offices. All the same, and in spite of the excellent case of the critic, the tower itself produces in the spectator a strong emotional impression—exactly the impression, by the way, which the gifted architect intended to convey.

CHICAGO TRIBUNE BUILDING, 1925

Michigan Boulevard
Howells & Hood

This building is an admirable monument of an unusually significant architectural competition. . . .

The competition proved influential in more ways than one. The more significant designs, published in book form, constituted a valuable collection of modern trends; it gave pictorial point to many a discussion, and found echoes, here and there, in subsequent building. The design which was awarded the second prize proved to be the passport to the American scene of Architect Eliel Saarinen, of Finland, whose presence has already influenced our most recent buildings and whose decided point of view may, before long, influence our larger civic projects. Finally, the tower which was actually erected added a gratifying silhouette to the lake front and has, without doubt, proved an inspiration to many.

HOLABIRD & ROCHE
ARCHITECTS
HUGH FERRISS. DEL.

11944

CHICAGO BOARD OF TRADE, 1930

141 West Jackson Boulevard
Holabird & Root

Chicago, in the last decade, has reared towers which, in pictorial interest, rival any of the metropolitan centers of the East. We have, of course, been long familiar with the sheer facade of the city which faces the lake across Michigan Boulevard; but a formation of quite different character has recently begun to crystallize definitely about the winding line of the river. . . .

An adequate suggestion of the most recent trend in Chicago is conveyed by the Board of Trade building whose strong, ascending mass stands out strikingly against the older buildings which are about it.

Left:
THE SHELTON HOTEL, 1924

525 Lexington Avenue
Arthur Loomis Harmon

The Shelton was one of the first of the very
large buildings to be erected after the enacting of the local "Zoning Laws"; that is to
say, it is one of the early examples of the
"set-back" type of structure. . . .

What a struggle some of the designers
made to force into the new "envelope" the
stylistic concepts with which their minds
were filled! In this case, it would appear that
the architect faced, without distaste, the volumes with which he was permitted to deal;
and modeled, with a single broad tool, the
mass which would most simply fill his space.

There is, in the building itself, something
reminiscent of the mountain. Many people
choose it as a residence, or frequent its upper terraces, because—known or unknown
to them—it evokes that undefinable sense of
satisfaction which man ever finds on the
slope of the pyramid or the mountainside.

The Shelton is already encircled by more
recent buildings which equal it only in
height; but there remains at least one point
of vantage from which its massive bulk can,
if only transitorily, still be glimpsed.

Right:
THE CHANIN BUILDING, 1929

122 East 42 Street
Sloan & Robertson

Of the 377 skyscrapers more than twenty
stories high, which stand in the United
States in 1929, 188 rise within the narrow
limits of New York City. Fifteen of these are
over five hundred feet tall; and of these fifteen, two—those illustrated on [this] and
the succeeding page—are exactly across the
street from each other.

When excavations were begun for the
earlier of these—the Chanin building—the
corner of Lexington and Forty-second
Street presented a fairly congested scene. . . .

Nevertheless, the deep excavation was
made and the lofty tower raised. The building, in itself, aroused lively interest. The architects had struck out boldly in their design: a yet bolder lobby was designed by the
owners themselves; the towering mass
presents an arresting spectacle when
seen . . . from the viewpoint of the present
drawing. . . .

Yet the flag pole was scarcely being
raised at this height, and added thousands of
people pouring onto Forty-second and
Lexington, before another great excavation
was begun directly across the street. . . .

THE CHRYSLER BUILDING, 1930

405 Lexington Avenue
William Van Alen

The excavation across the street proved to be the beginning of the Chrysler building which was to overtop the Chanin—rising, in fact, to considerably over eight hundred feet.

In the view which is here shown, we are looking eastward, away from the city: and from this viewpoint the tower looms up freely against the low buildings of the East Side, the river and the horizontal stretches of Long Island. Were we to view it from the opposite direction, it would, however, merge into the great mass of Grand Central skyscrapers (although its unusual terminal curve would still surmount the whole composition) and one might have some foreboding of its effect upon the congestion of Forty-second and Lexington.

It required a considerably more detailed drawing than the one at hand to delineate the many novel effects which, in this design, the architect has ingeniously produced in the fenestration, the brick work and other details which are quite apparent in the building itself; the intention in this sketch is simply to convey an impression of the extreme dimensions which are involved.

THE EMPIRE STATE BUILDING, 1931

350 Fifth Avenue
Shreve, Lamb & Harmon

Those who recall the appearance of the Waldorf-Astoria hotel will find, in the office building which is about to take its place, a vivid illustration of the contemporary trend in architecture.

To some, no doubt, the heavy masonry arches and the mosque-like domes of the older structure will seem the more appealing—standing, for them, as it must, for the familiar charm of older days and presenting no challenging or disturbing thought.

Yet many will experience a strong emotion in the presence of the vast steps and the sheer ascending planes of the structure now arising. In its forthright structural simplicity, its scale, and its power, it definitely announces the coming of a new order.

DAILY NEWS BUILDING, 1930

220 East 42 Street
Howells & Hood

"A circular space, 150 feet in circumference—to be enclosed by a wall of black glass which rises, unbroken by any windows, to a black glass ceiling; in the center of a brass-inlaid floor, a cup-shaped well from which light—the sole illumination of the room—is to stream. Bathed in this light, a ten-foot terrestrial globe is to revolve—its even revolutions reflected darkly in the night-like ceiling above."

The foregoing specification might seem to point, perhaps, to a hall dedicated to some high scientific or even religious idea: it would scarcely be taken to refer to the entrance lobby of a news-paper and office building. Yet just this lobby, as described, stands within a stone's throw of Grand Central Terminal.

Why is so bizarre a design included in so utilitarian a building? Has it merely a publicity value? What effect, if any, will it have upon the thousands of people who hurry in and out every day?

It can scarcely be doubted that the sight of it will give them pause . . . they may experience at least passing realization of the situation of their own planet—revolving, at that very instant, in the black crystal of space. . . .

Left:
PHILADELPHIA SAVINGS FUND SOCIETY BUILDING, 1932

12 South 12th Street
Howe & Lescaze

There are designers to whom . . . the very absence of adornment is itself a recommendation. From them we may expect buildings exhibiting a certain starkness and even nakedness—those qualities which are, indeed, the norm for all newly-arisen forms.

Right:
LEVER HOUSE, 1952

390 Park Avenue
Skidmore, Owings & Merrill

While it is the sleekness and shimmer that have won Lever House a certain popularity, these are hardly the most important gains, architecturally. More important are the facts that instead of filling the three-dimensional "envelope" to the full, as in the "wedding cake" type, thousands of cubic yards of space are salvaged with all their light and air; and that by opening the ground floor to the street, the public gains hundreds of square yards to walk through or linger in: a breathing space with vistas, giving us a modern version of the ancient plaza.

PRELIMINARY SCHEME FOR ROCKEFELLER CENTER, 1929

48th to 51st Streets, between Fifth and Sixth Avenues
Corbett, Harrison & McMurray
Rockefeller Center is an outstanding and famous example of teamwork. With remarkably few real changes within the team, the prolonged task of assembling three entire midtown Manhattan blocks into one unified design has been steadily pushed forward since 1929.

EASTERN AIRLINES BUILDING, 1939

10 Rockefeller Plaza
Reinhard & Hofmeister, Wallace K. Harrison and J. André
Fouilhoux

Among the "ingredients" of today's architecture is glass. It is often said that the area of glass in our contemporary buildings is becoming excessively large. Actually, the large area here depicted was partially covered by an interior screen after the structure had been built. This screen was later removed.

What attracted my eye to this particular scene was not the transparency of the glass but its changing reflections. The next time you look through a plate-glass window at a display of merchandise, you might shift the focus, look at the *glass*, and study the always fascinating world of reflections.

The overglazed surfaces of some recent commercial buildings have been criticized by neighbors who, naturally enough, do not care to live in light reflected as from a mirror. But notice how some of the recent metal-and-glass facades succeed in reflecting more quietly the images of near-by buildings, of passing crowds, or of clouds—and they reflect in a way that enlivens and enhances the over-all architectural effect.

GENERAL VIEW, UNITED NATIONS HEADQUARTERS, NEW YORK, 1947–1953

First Avenue, between 42nd and 48th Streets
International Committee of Architects: Wallace K. Harrison, Chairman

This picture, based on blueprints and on a sketch made from a helicopter poised over the site, was published on the day the cornerstone was laid. There are only a few details in which it does not agree with the shapes of the buildings as later erected. To watch a dream come true, to see rising in metal and stone what had existed in imagination only, this is an experience well known to all who are in any way connected with the practice of architecture. . . .

In 1958 or thereafter, when not only the buildings will have been completed but also the carefully planned landscaping, if you will go to the extreme northeast corner of the terrace overhanging the East River, lean against the shipshape railing, and look back at this world capital standing before you in its entirety, you will get (what the premature talk during construction did not give, and what drawings can never give) an understanding of the simple and strong conception that the Director of Planning and the Planning Staff have had in mind from the beginning.

LINCOLN CENTER FOR THE PERFORMING ARTS, NEW YORK, 1962–1968

Broadway to Amsterdam Avenue, 62nd to 66th Streets
Buildings shown in the drawing are (left to right):
New York State Theater, Philip C. Johnson and Richard Foster, 1964
Metropolitan Opera House, Wallace K. Harrison, 1966
Avery Fisher Hall (originally Philharmonic Hall), Max Abramovitz, 1962
In a letter from Venice in the summer of 1961, Hugh Ferriss wrote to Max Abramovitz:
Having paced this Piazza by sunlight and moonlight for the past 10 days, I agree with the opinion—attributed to you by the *N. Y. Times*—that here is Architecture's masterpiece. And despite differences in forms & dimensions, the similarity in plot plan to Lincoln Center is inescapable; . . .

Your responsibility is handsome and immense. Naturally, no one wants a replica of San Marco. . . . But a true designer *can* "reincarnate" a dateless spirit in new and viable forms. Even a campanile (sadly lacking in Lincoln Center except in one early sketch) could be devised (tall & slender) in an abstract "wire sculpture."

When I was last in New York, the Philharmonic was taking form in great delicacy and strength. Congratulations!

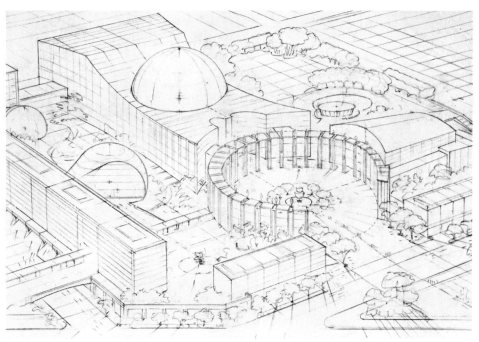

99

NORRIS DAM, TENNESSEE, 1936

Architects and Engineers of the Tennessee Valley Authority

One learns, in the Tennessee Valley, names that are famous in the history of man-made structures (Walt Whitman would have enjoyed invoking them): Pickwick, Wheeler, Chickamauga, Norris, Hiwassee, Cherokee. It is from the air that one gets the full story; the remodeling of a whole valley, an architecture for a region. The air age gives a new facade to architecture; so far as I know, artists have yet to portray it.

100

CHEROKEE DAM, TENNESSEE, 1942

Architects and Engineers of the Tennessee Valley Authority
I have seen no more massive evidence of this nation's power in buildings than in the work of the United States Bureau of Reclamation and the Tennessee Valley Authority. My acquaintance with the latter began one October day in 1941 when Roland Wank, Chief Architect at that time, explained . . . how the plans, from inception, passed regularly back and forth between the Authority's architectural and its engineering staff. . . . The integration is obvious in the visible results; vast usefulness combined with deeply impressive forms.

Right:
HOOVER DAM, ARIZONA-NEVADA LINE, 1936

United States Bureau of Reclamation
Gordon B. Kauffmann, Consulting Architect
Driving away from Hoover Dam, via Las Vegas, the route lay not far from an officially sequestered area where is being generated power of a different order, designed for a different purpose; one looked for the sudden flash, the rising mushroom-shaped cloud. Modern science, which knows no national boundaries, has thrust into man's fallible hands unprecedented power: power in building, power in destroying.

GRAND COULEE DAM, WASHINGTON, 1942

United States Bureau of Reclamation
Gordon B. Kauffmann, Consulting Architect

Turning north from the Snake River into a landscape as wild as the moon's and seemingly as uninhabited, we came suddenly upon the largest structure ever reared by man.

We inspected the dam and the clean-cut town that had grown alongside it; later we slept in one of the modern cabins next to the white, leviathan mass. Through the hot summer nights the cabins are cooled by water from the dam—each roof cooled by its own watery plume spraying in the moonlight like Moby Dick's.

The second day, we went down to the lowest interior reaches of the dam, with a photographer whose prints I have kept as evidence that in these two drawings the size of the structures has not been overstated through the familiar device of understating the size of human figures. While I was making the sketch, the turbine was being assembled, and the large section of pipe lowered into place. A photograph made simultaneously is my proof that the workers are drawn at a height of exactly five feet, ten inches.

PRELIMINARY FOR DRWG OF DAM FOR POWER IN BUILDINGS

SHASTA DAM, CALIFORNIA, 1943

United States Bureau of Reclamation
Gordon B. Kauffmann, Consulting Architect
[The] form [of a Zapotec Indian structure] came back to mind when, among the mountains
of northern California, we saw Shasta Dam. [The two structures] provide examples of similar forms and diametrically opposed functions. For Shasta unceremoniously makes available the power of five generators of 75,000-kilowatt capacity each, brings water to a million
acres of potentially fertile land, remakes the map of California, and works effectively for
abundant life.

RED ROCKS PARK, COLORADO

It is a certain spot on the map, . . . going west across the Nebraska-Colorado plain. I remember it as it looked at that moment, shortly after dawn, when the eastward-rolling earth leisurely lifts over the horizon the first entrancing escarpments of the Rocky Mountains. There, it seems, rises a monumental exit from all familiar cares.

Preliminary sketch for Red Rocks Amphitheater, 1942

Following page:
RED ROCKS AMPHITHEATER, 1942

Burnham Hoyt, Architect

There is one thing certain: architecture has never been called a destructive art. Nowhere does a nation's constructive genius show itself more plainly, more simply, or more often than in its buildings. Architects, by nature as by training, are on the constructive side. Their affirmative influence has been felt in the Capitol dome seen in Washington, the solemn shaft seen farther down the Mall, or in a home of one's own seen across fields at dusk. It can be more widely felt in the plans for better housing, offices, and plants, better neighborhoods, towns, and regions. Others may teach or preach synthesis in man's life; architects can build it into his surroundings, and through the massive influence of environment can directly affect his life. Such long-term, constructive tasks, as compared to the sudden, destructive ones, will always be the harder to launch and to sustain, always the less appealing to publicity and propaganda. Architects will never be headlined along with the authors and agents of planned destruction. But there is something to be said for the purely creative impulse. It is a sign of an evolutionary scheme in whose further possibilities we may devoutly believe. It is a mark of man at his manliest. And it is the least obscure reflection of his Creator.

PERISPHERE AND TRYLON DURING CONSTRUCTION, 1939

New York World's Fair, 1939–1940
Wallace K. Harrison and J. André Fouil-houx

The exposition was concerned with "building the world of tomorrow"—not by fanciful prophecy, but by exhibition of the existing tools with which, of necessity, that world must be built. . . . Scores of buildings by the various designers were erected, and in combination they gave a lively background to the theme; however, it was necessary to conceive one focal structure that would unmistakably represent it. . . . After many experimental stages, and lively meetings with the Board of Design, there emerged [a] structure shaped like the world, with its pointer toward tomorrow. . . . Like the other Fair structures, this one was demolished in 1941, but the image serves to recall a theme that the world was to think of ruefully in the war years so soon to follow.

Preceding page:
JOHNSON WAX COMPANY BUILDING,
RACINE, WISCONSIN, 1936–1939

Frank Lloyd Wright

Wright has often spoken of. . . "organic" architecture, and his Johnson Building (a large shell) exemplifies it. At first approach, the exterior, lacking conventional windows, may seem enigmatic—a shape without a purpose—but the apparent mystery is cleared up if one goes inside.

Above:
INTERIOR, JOHNSON WAX COMPANY BUILDING, 1936–1939

Inside the Johnson Building one perceives the actual construction and appreciates the ample, natural lighting through the roof. It is precisely at this point that a criticism is sometimes made: couldn't this space have been enclosed more expertly and economically by omitting the unique columns and running simple girders straight across? The question is typical of the structural engineer and the cost accountant, and shows up their understanding of the word "function."

Actually, a large number of office workers spend almost a third of their daily existence in this room. There are sound reasons for making office space pleasant. The function of a building is more than the sum of the mechanical jobs performed by its various structural members. Consciously or unconsciously, people's lives are influenced by environment, and for most of us a large portion of environment is made up of buildings. . . . A building's chief function is related to its effect on people's lives. Employees in the Johnson Building stated to me that they found it an inspiring place in which to work.

PRELIMINARY SCHEME,
GENERAL MOTORS TECHNICAL CENTER,
DETROIT, MICHIGAN, 1945

Saarinen, Swanson, and Saarinen
A section of the General Motors Technical Center as the design in its early stages was being formulated during Eliel Saarinen's lifetime. . . . For me, the drawing serves to recall the invaluable, daily conversations with the elder Saarinen, whose firmness and sagacity are sometimes attained by great architects in their latter years, and whose humor and modesty they usually never attain.

GRAIN ELEVATOR, KANSAS CITY, MISSOURI, 1939

Horner & Wyatt, Engineers

Some reference, at least, should be made to one of the most familiar forms of the American scene: the massed concrete cylinders of the grain elevators. They are, of course, outstanding features of the Buffalo lake front; there is a handsome composition of them at Battle Creek, Michigan; they are perhaps seen at their best at Duluth.

One night, driving south near Shakopee, Minnesota, a vast bulk rose slowly out of the dark plain, and in its isolated, columnar, Egyptian dignity it stood as an anonymous monument to the nation's natural resources and abundant power.

All of these elevators are good structural testaments. The one in Missouri, shown here, happens to be a particularly large and busy installation.

OHIO STEEL FOUNDRY, LIMA, 1939

Albert Kahn Associates, Architects and Engineers

There is no attempt in this building at monumentality in the usual sense, that of masonry massiveness. What is presented to the eye is not mass so much as volume—enclosed space, or "controlled environment." There is glass where glass is needed; the simple curtain-wall completes the envelope; the straightforward steel structure is visible; and there is an abundance of working space, light, and air. It is the very lack of architectural ostentation that makes the building such a lucid monument when seen at the site.

FORD AIRCRAFT ENGINE PLANT, DEARBORN, MICHIGAN, 1941

Giffels & Vallett and L. Rosetti, Architects
By contrast [to the Ohio Steel Foundry], you may find the emphatic horizontal in this plant either arresting or arbitrary according to your way of thinking.

TRIBOROUGH BRIDGE ANCHORAGE, NEW YORK, 1936

Triborough Bridge and Tunnel Authority;
Aymar Embury II, Consulting Architect

Many people think of bridges as not being in the category of architecture. Actually, they well exemplify the architectural problem of combining structural utility and structural beauty. . . . By leaving out many details that would have been caught by the camera, I have emphasized the lines and planes which, at the site, give a sense of strong organization to this simple, utilitarian anchorage.

PROPOSED ALTERATIONS, METROPOLITAN MUSEUM OF ART, NEW YORK,
1946

Robert B. O'Connor and Aymar Embury II

In 1946—the seventy-fifth anniversary of the Metropolitan Museum of Art—its Director,
Francis Henry Taylor, its trustees, the Mayor, and other city officials launched the drive for
large-scale alterations and additions to the famous edifice. From architectural drawings that
were mainly concerned with new wings surrounding three large, new courts, the sketch
[above] is selected to note the fact that even in the older and more familiar portions of the
building, many stone moldings and projections, once esteemed architectural necessities,
are earmarked for removal. In short, the remodeling of the Museum will exemplify the
trend toward simplification.

TALIESIN-IN-ARIZONA, SCOTTSDALE, 1938

Frank Lloyd Wright

I have already mentioned an indefinable element that makes some builders "master builders." During a day-long contemplation of Taliesin, that isolated work of art in the desert,
it seemed likely that this element is love. Some architects design with love and some do
not. The latter may have the gift of preaching theories; they may fathom all scientific
truths; but though they speak with the tongues of men and of angels, yet have not love,
their designs become "as sounding brass or a tinkling cymbal."

BOMBPROOF SHELTER, NEW YORK, A 1942 PROPOSAL

The late George J. Atwell, whose companies had successfully carried out many major excavations, including tunnels under the Hudson, at one time proposed an extensive operation in the Palisades of that river. As announced at the time, this "underground city" would serve various purposes, including storage, safe-deposit vaults, and certain types of manufacturing. It was not so widely announced that the main purpose was to provide, under two hundred feet of solid rock, bombproof shelters for the inhabitants of a city with which there would be direct subway connections. . . .

Estimates of cost, construction timetables, and more detailed drawings were submitted to federal and state authorities, whose replies were varied and interesting. A general reaction expressed was that massive attacks on United States cities were "out of the question." That was in December, *1942*.

Since they are no longer out of the question, the problems involved have been reapproached from other angles. . . . If the nations have accepted as a legitimate objective in war the wholesale annihilation of civilian populations, is it in order to match blueprints and budgets for a huge war plant with blueprints and budgets for a huge system of civilian defense? Can the blueprints be drawn, and is the money forthcoming? Will real estate interests allow the razing of wide swaths of valuable property for any purpose whatever? Will the populations of large cities join in an orderly, gradual exodus to scattered communities, or will they take a chance on a last-minute, fatal route? Will people live underground?

Following page:
NATIONAL AIRPORT, WASHINGTON, D.C., 1941

Public Buildings Administration
Howard L. Cheney, Consulting Architect
Louis A. Simon, Supervising Architect
When perspectives are drawn to assist in designing a proposed building . . . the draftsman is concerned solely with the mass, volume, and shape of the structure itself; the surroundings and the atmosphere are for the moment unimportant, the draftsmanship is usually on the abstract side. By contrast, this drawing aims at recording an impression received at the actual site from an existing building. It is drawn as though it were seen at night because that was the case. Artificial light was coming from within the building and was reflected from the planes on the apron. The moon appeared as shown, directly above the pointer, the Washington Monument. Many people were about and they seemed to be looking at the same things I was. In short, the aim, here, is not to show how buildings look on drafting boards to theoretical designers but how they look in actuality to ordinary people.

Hugh Ferriss

NOTES

Published sources for the Ferriss illustrations in this book are included in Notes for the Drawings. Articles and books mentioned in the Introduction or Notes are more fully described in the Bibliography. Abbreviations used here are HF (for Hugh Ferriss), *PB (Power in Buildings)*, and *MT (Metropolis of Tomorrow)*.

INTRODUCTION

1. HF graduated from the St. Louis Manual Training School in 1906. Operated by Washington University from 1879 to 1917, the school offered a three-year program of "manual and mental exercises" (from the school catalog, 1882).

2. HF, "Architectural Rendering," *Encyclopaedia Britannica*, 1961. First published in 1929, this article was rewritten by the author for the 1961 printing, and material that he by that time considered "of interest to specialists only" was deleted, including a detailed description of his personal approach to rendering.

3. In the 1920s HF served as a design consultant to city planning groups in Pittsburgh and St. Louis and to the preliminary design board of the Chicago World's Exposition of 1933. He lectured on design and rendering at Yale, Columbia University, the University of Pennsylvania, and Pratt Institute. Manufacturers of steel, terra cotta, and cement used his drawings in advertisements. See especially the series published by the American Institute of Steel Construction in *Pencil Drawings of High Buildings and Bridges* and in the *American Architect* (April 1930 to March 1931). A number of these drawings were exhibited at the Roerich Museum in 1932. See Bibliography: Art Exhibits; Books.

4. HF, "Civic Architecture of the Immediate Future," *Arts and Decoration*, November 1922, p. 13.

5. Review by Ralph Flint of the Anderson Galleries exhibition (see note 31) in *The Christian Science Monitor*, Apr. 23, 1925, p. 8.

6. "Ferriss' Future-Perfect," *Time*, May 18, 1942, pp. 42–43.

7. Catalog note by Adolf Placzek for "Architects for a New Nation, 1776–1976," a Bicentennial exhibition of renderings from the Avery Library, Columbia University.

8. Note on a Piranesi exhibition at the Morgan Library, *Architectural Forum*, March 1949, p. 64.

9. William Jordy sees HF drawings as "blurred images" *(American Buildings and Their Architects*, p. 430). Rem Koolhaas in *Delirious New York* describes HF as "the Master of Darkness" (p. 232) whose "vague and ambiguous" drawings were designed to "stimulate confusion while paying lip-service to clarification" (pp. 98–100).

10. Letter of Sept. 29, 1926, to Gordon W.C. Holt, a British writer on rendering techniques.

11. From an interview with Ernest Burden at his New York office in the fall of 1976.

12. HF, "Some Testimony from One Who Renders," *Architectural Record*, August 1956, p. 9.

13. *Encyclopaedia Britannica* article of 1961. See note 2.

14. Ibid.

15. Quotations on the psychological aspects of architectural rendering and on the delineator's task are from HF's *Encyclopaedia Britannica* article of 1929. Comment on the "individual existence" of buildings from the artist's talk on "Truth in Architectural Rendering," *American Institute of Architects Journal*, March 1925, p. 99.

16. Information on rendering "factories" from Ernest Burden. For comment on architectural rendering today, see Ada Louise Huxtable, "Modern Architecture In Question," *New York Review of Books*, Nov. 27, 1975, p. 6; also Paul Goldberger, "Architectural Drawings Make Comeback to Respectibility," *New York Times*, Sept. 22, 1977, Section III, p. 16.

17. The Beaux-Arts influence on architectural education in the United States reached its peak between 1900 and 1925. The School of Architecture at Washington University was formed in 1899 as an adjunct to the School of Engineering and did not achieve independence until 1910.

18. "Architecture: General Outline of Instruction," *Washington University Record*, November 1906–1907.

19. Wilbur Tyson Trueblood, instructor in architecture, "The French Influence on Architectural Design in America," *Washington University Record*, April 1911, pp. 27–28. Courtesy Archives, Washington University Libraries.

20. *PB*, p. 6.

21. HF was introduced to Cass Gilbert (1859–1934) by Franklin Ferriss, his father, who was then serving as a judge on the state supreme court of Missouri. HF's first employer, Louis LaBeaume (1873–1961), also was well acquainted with Gilbert, and both men were associated with the Louisiana Purchase Centennial of 1904: LaBeaume as Chief of Design, Gilbert as architect of the recently restored St. Louis Art Museum.

22. Charles Dana Gibson, chairman of pictorial publicity, Committee on Public Information, to George Creel, the committee chairman: "This will be handed to you by Mr. Hugh Ferriss, who comes to me highly recommended by Mr. Cass Gilbert. His work is first class and speaks for itself." Letter of Dec. 29, 1917.

23. Frank Chouteau Brown, "A New Note in Architectural Rendering: The Work of Mr. Hugh Ferriss," *Architectural Review* (Boston), August 1918, p. 21. In 1919, a one-man show of 34 HF drawings (shipyards, Liberty Loan Parades, New York streets and buildings) was held at the Paint-Box Gallery, then located at 43 Washington Square South, and a series of wartime illustrations appeared in *Harper's Magazine*. For a brief summary of HF's career between 1915 and 1920, see *Pencil Points*, December 1920, p. 25.

24. Recollections of Harvey Corbett (1873–1954) from a Ferriss speech at a memorial exhibition of Corbett's work held at The Architectural League on Feb. 17, 1955. The Bush Terminal Building, completed by Corbett & Helmle in 1917, held "the same high place of architectural esteem in the Forty-Second Street district as does the Woolworth Building in lower Manhattan" *(Architectural Forum*, Oct. 20, 1920, p. 509).

25. For background on the Corbett-Ferriss proposals for elevated sidewalks, see captions and notes for drawings on pages 48–49 and 68–69.

26. A full-size replica of King Solomon's temple was designed by Corbett for the Philadelphia Sesquicentennial of 1926 in collaboration with John Wesley Kelchner, a biblical scholar. HF drawings of the project were reproduced in a 1925 publicity brochure with text by Kelchner and were featured in the *New York Times*, Sept. 6, 1925, p. 45, and in *Pencil Points*, November 1925, pp. 69–86. The proposal appears never to have been realized. See Corbett comment, *New York Times*, Nov. 18, 1926, p. 20.

27. The Equitable Building of 1915 (Ernest R. Graham, Architect) was the world's largest in total area—1.2 million square feet—until the advent of the Empire State in 1931. Public protest on completion of the massive hulk, still standing at 120 Broadway, led to adoption of the first zoning laws in 1916.

28. HF comments on the zoning ordinance that restricted the height of buildings are taken from "The New Architecture," *New York Times Book Review and Magazine*, Mar. 19, 1922, pp. 8–9, 27. Under these regulations, buildings were permitted to rise on their lot lines only to specified heights; above this, they were stepped back within a line drawn from the center of the street through the top of the wall on the lot line. The height of the wall was based on the width of the street which the building faced, in accordance with a formula that divided New York into five zones of varying height allowances.

29. Ibid. HF's enthusiasm for the zoning laws was shared by many contemporaries. For a notable example see Fiske Kimball, *American Architecture*, pp. 221–224.

30. In "Civic Architecture of the Immediate Future," HF predicted that "within a generation the congested areas of large cities will be razed" *(Arts and Decoration*, November 1922, p. 13).

31. The Anderson Galleries exhibition was divided into three parts: "A study of the nature of the masses resulting from the present New York Zoning Law"; "Studies of buildings designed by various architects, illustrating contemporary developments under the Zoning Law"; and "Studies of the Future City." A number of these drawings were later reproduced in *MT*. See also Bibliography: Art Reviews.

32. The Tercentenary Pictorial Pageant of New York City was timed to coincide with the opening of a new building for the John Wanamaker store at Ninth Street and Broadway (later destroyed by fire). In October 1925, the Great Rotunda of the old building was given over to an historical display of the "Titan City" that featured a 75-foot high painting on transparent silk by the Hungarian designer, Willy Pogany. Ferriss's murals were part of a display in the new building that also included a "Grand Canyon" of miniature model skyscrapers of the future, executed by Harvey Corbett, who served as a director of the show. In a letter to HF of Aug. 13, 1925, Corbett remarked: "I think this is a most interesting opportunity to get some one to pay for the futuristic ideas we have discussed." See also Frontispiece caption and Bibliography: Art Reviews.

33. Quotations are from "The New New York," *Vanity Fair*, December 1925, p. 67; a letter to HF from John Mead Howells, following the opening of the Anderson Galleries show on April 13 of that year; and a review of the exhibition in *American Art News*, April 18, p. 7.

34. Approximately two-thirds of the 60 drawings reproduced in *MT* were publicized some years before as straightforward projections of the zoning law. Nearly all the illustrations in the final "Imaginary Metropolis" section of the book were drawn especially for that purpose.

35. It is an ironic footnote to HF's work of the 1920s that drawings intended by the artist as caricatures of the contemporary architectural scene are often misread today as evidence of support for trends in architecture that he in fact opposed. See, for example, captions and notes for "Overhead Traffic Ways" (page 44) and "Crowding Towers" (page 45).

36. *MT*, pp. 16–17.

37. *MT*, pp. 109–110.

38. For HF comments on the traffic situation in 1929, see caption and note for the elevated sidewalk illustrations shown on pages 48–49.

39. Of 59 drawings displayed at the Roerich Museum in 1932 (see Bibliography: Art Reviews), 12 were illustrations for a "forthcoming book, now in preparation, which proposes a city replanning based upon . . . the recognition, preservation and encouragement of human values in an age increasingly mechanistic" (from the show catalog). See caption and note for "Proposal to Separate Pedestrian from Vehicular Traffic" on pages 68–69.

40. Reference to airports near the business district from *MT*, p. 138; to landing "shelves" for airplanes, *MT*, p. 64.

41. Although HF deplored New York's lack of plan, the "architectural confectionary" of its buildings, and the financial greed of its property owners *(MT*, p. 16), he dismissed proposals for decentralization as a "mere dream" *(MT*, p. 59) and believed that "the mature and responsible approach to the problem . . . is to replan and rebuild" *(PB*, plate 28).

42. Lewis Mumford on "moonstruck sketches"; *The New Yorker*, Oct. 22, 1949, p. 106; on HF visions of the future, "The Sacred City," *New Republic*, Jan. 27, 1926, pp. 270–271. For comment on HF's influence on architecture of the '20s see Claude Bragdon, "Skyscrapers," *American Mercury*, March 1931, reprinted in Bragdon's *The Frozen Fountain*; Sheldon Cheney, *The New World Architecture*, p. 144; also reviews of *MT*.

43. Statistics cited by HF in *MT*, p. 72.

44. G.H. Edgell, *The American Architecture of Today* (New York: Charles Scribner's Sons, 1928), p. 356.

45. Lewis Mumford, "Magnified Impotence," *New Republic*, Dec. 22, 1926, p. 139.

46. *MT*, p. 80.

47. Lewis Mumford, "Mr. Rockefeller's Center," *The New Yorker*, Dec. 23, 1933, pp. 29–30. William Jordy also draws a parallel between HF drawings and early plans for Rockefeller Center in *The Impact of European Modernism in the Mid-Twentieth Century*, Vol. 4, *American Buildings and Their Architects* (New York: Doubleday, 1972), pp. 65–67.

48. HF on architecture of the Roosevelt era: *Newsweek*, May 11, 1942, p. 68; *Time*, May 18, 1942, p. 42.

49. The first Arnold W. Brunner award granted by The Architectural League was divided between HF and artist Leon V. Solon *(New York Times*, Dec. 25, 1940, p. 28).

50. American Academy award ceremonies of May 12, 1943.

51. The Mayor's Committee on Plan and Scope was headed by Robert Moses, with Gilmore D. Clarke as chairman of the committee's Board of Design. HF drawings of the project, together with models of the proposed buildings, were presented to the UN General Assembly in September 1946 *(PB*, text for plates 33–34). See Robert Moses, "Natural and Proper Home of the United Nations," *New York Times Magazine*, Oct. 20, 1946 (cover drawing and five HF illustrations of the Flushing Meadows proposal).

52. William Zeckendorf was one of the city's most aggressive real estate tycoons until the failure of his firm, Webb & Knapp, in 1965. Other architects he employed at various times included I.M. Pei, William Lescaze, and Le Corbusier.

53. *New York Times*, Dec. 12, 1946, p. 1.

54. "Charette" is reproduced in *PB*, plate 39. HF was one of a dozen consultants present at the first conference called by Director of Planning Wallace K. Harrison on Jan. 23, 1947. His contract specified that he provide in-progress studies and final presentation drawings of the project and participate in design meetings. By the end of 1948, HF had completed close to 300 studies of progressive stages in the design of the UN headquarters. A final Ferriss study of this project was a sketch of the UN Library designed by Harrison & Abramovitz *(New York Times*, Sept. 30, 1959, p. 1).

55. For comment on HF's role in carrying out this project, see Edith Iglauer, "The UN Builds Its Home," *Harper's Magazine*, December 1947, p. 566; Howard Robertson, "The American Scene," *Journal of the Royal Institute of British Architects*, April 1948. For the artist's own view of his UN assignment, see *PB*, text for plates 33–44; also, "Designing the U.N. Headquarters," *Journal, Royal Architectural Institute of Canada*, vol. 25 (March 1948), pp. 69–80 (20 illustrations).

56. An outline of HF's work for "various groups concerned with city architecture": Director of the Municipal Art Society of New York, 1946–1947; Architect member of the City Art Commission, 1947–1950; Allied Professional Member of the National Sculpture Society, 1944; Associate (1955) and Academician (1960) of the National Academy of Design.

A member of The Architectural League of New York after 1921, HF was president of that group from 1943–1945. He received its first prize awarded for architectural rendering (1930); two Birch Burdette Long prizes for rendering (1934 and 1944); two Arnold W. Brunner Scholarship awards (1940 and 1951); and the President's Medal (1941) "for stimulating that interest in the arts for which the League stands," through his work as chairman of the League's Exhibitions Committee.

HF was elected a Fellow of the New York chapter of the American Institute of Architects in 1950 and served as president of the chapter from 1952–1954.

57. Letter from HF to his father on Nov. 18, 1923 (see quotations from this letter in text, page 23).

58. "Frank Lloyd Wright and Hugh Ferriss Discuss This Modern Architecture," *Architectural Forum*, November 1930, pp. 535–538.

59. *The Metropolis of Tomorrow* and Le Corbusier's *The City of Tomorrow* (New York: Payson & Clarke, 1929)—an English translation of his *Urbanisme* of 1924—were recommended as ideal Christmas presents for architecture buffs *(Saturday Review of Literature*, Dec. 7, 1929, p. 542). A likeness between proposals put forward by both men was noted by various reviewers at the time; see, for example, Sheldon Cheney, *New World Architecture*, pp. 81–82, 400; Claude Bragdon, *Frozen Fountain*, p. 34. Joshua C. Taylor, however, sees a "dramatic" difference in viewpoint between the two [*America as Art* (Washington, D.C.: Smithsonian Institution Press, 1976), pp. 192–193]. Le Corbusier himself touched on that difference in *La Ville Radieuse* (Paris: L'Architecture d'Aujourd'hui, 1935), in which he includes, without attribution, the four HF zoning "envelope" drawings of 1922 to illustrate "conflicting spiritual attitudes" between French and American architects (p. 133).

60. Le Corbusier on New York: *Quand les Cathédrales étaient Blanches* (Paris: Plon, 1937), pp. 55–56

61. Peter Blake, "The Masonry Age," *New York Times Book Review*, Sept. 27, 1953, p. 43.

62. HF on "civil war" in architecture: "The Impact of Science and Materialism on Art Today," *Journal of the American Institute of Architects*,

July 1954, p. 4. On lack of synthesis in architecture: *PB*, pp. 12–13. On architecture's goal, see "Red Rocks Amphitheater," *PB*, plate 68.

63. *Christian Science Monitor*, Apr. 23, 1925, p. 8 (see note 5).

64. For a retrospective look at the skyscraper city foreseen in the 1920s by HF and others, see Winston Weisman, "Skyscrapers: The Return to Earth," *Architectural Review*, March 1950, p. 202.

DRAWINGS

The published sources mentioned here refer only to drawings reproduced in this book or to renderings or sketches of related subjects. There is no attempt here or in the Bibliography to include all of the hundreds of Ferriss illustrations in various books, magazines, and newspapers, nor does this list provide more than an outline of projects with which he was associated. As with the work of so many architects and professional delineators, numerous Ferriss drawings have been lost or destroyed or—for lack of time and funds with which to catalogue them—lie buried in various library and museum collections awaiting future discovery. Owners of still extant originals shown here are named in the Photography Credits, with the Avery Library of Columbia University heading the list as owner of more than three hundred Ferriss drawings and sketches.

DREAMS (1922-1932)
The Lure of the City (pages 42–43)
Drawn 1925, this was one of four Ferriss drawings included in a Bicentennial exhibition of American art at the National Collection of Fine Arts, Washington, D.C., in a section titled "The Image of Urban Optimism." For a comparison of HF's work with that of other artists and designers of the 1920s, see Joshua C. Taylor, *America as Art*, pp. 192–194; also Stephen Zoll, "Superville," *Massachusetts Review*, pp. 449–450 (Ill.).

Overhead Traffic Ways (page 44)
This caricature of proposals put forward by others for a "network of aerial traffic bridges" has been confused by various critics with proposals made by HF himself. When Winston Weisman wrote that HF in the 1920s had envisaged skyscraper cities "composed of gigantic structures tied together by super skyways," the artist promptly replied: "My distaste for such an unpleasant conception is recorded at some length in my book, *The Metropolis of Tomorrow*." (Winston Weisman, "The Rise and Rise of the Skyscraper," *New York Times Magazine*, Sept. 20, 1953, p. 14; HF letter to the editor, Oct. 4, 1953.) His protest was in vain, however; similar misconceptions have been expressed in books by Cheney; Conrads and Sperlich; Fitch; and Wolf.

Crowding Towers (page 45)
First published in "New York of the Future," *Vanity Fair*, September 1926, p. 84; also *Architect and Building News*, Aug. 9, 1929. Like the drawing on the previous page, "Crowding Towers" is a warning, not a recommendation, and portrays the logical outcome of building endless rows of skyscrapers, side by side, in the least pos-

sible space. Ferriss himself advocated widely spaced, multiblock buildings of maximum height.

Reversion to Past Styles (pages 46-47)
The caption is quoted from a 1922 Ferriss article, "Civic Architecture of the Immediate Future" (*Arts and Decoration*, November, pp. 12–13), in which this tongue-in-cheek projection of eclectic style superimposed on setback buildings first appeared. See also George MacAdam, "Vision of New York That May Be," *New York Times Magazine*, May 25, 1924, p. 2.

A Proposal by Harvey Wiley Corbett. Elevated Sidewalks (pages 48-49)
The rendering appears on the cover of *Pencil Points* of June 1926; there are related sketches in a Corbett article on "The Problem of Traffic Congestion and a Solution" (*Architectural Forum*, March 1927, p. 200). First put forward by Corbett in 1923, this proposal was designed to increase the traffic capacity of New York "up to and even beyond 700%" (quote is from *The Building of the City*, pp. 309–310, a Regional Plan of New York, study of 1931, in which these and other HF drawings appear).

A Proposal by Raymond Hood: Apartments on Bridges (pages 50-51)
Illustration for a 1925 article by Orrick Johns, based on an interview with Raymond Hood, "Bridge Homes: A New Vision of the City," *New York Times Magazine*, Feb. 22, 1925, p. 5. For comment on the drawing see *Christian Science Monitor*, Apr. 23, 1925, p. 8. In spite of its fantastic air, Hood's plan was a sober attempt to provide homes for 3 million people and to bring Manhattan's office workers closer to their jobs by incorporating apartment houses into bridges leading into the city across the Hudson and East rivers (see Hood on "New York of the Future," *Creative Arts*, August 1931). Similar proposals were put forward in the 1920s by other architects from Chicago to Paris. For background, see Conrads and Sperlich, *The Architecture of Fantasy*.

Zoning Envelopes: First through Fourth Stages (pages 52-53)
First published by HF in "The New Architecture," *New York Times Book Review and Magazine*, Mar. 19, 1922, pp. 8–9 (for description of this article, see Introduction, pages 30–31); also used by Corbett in "Zoning and the Envelope of the Building," *Pencil Points*, April 1923, pp. 15–18. Reproduced and exhibited here and abroad from 1925 on, these drawings are still standard illustrations of the 1916 zoning law in New York.

Buildings in the Modeling (page 54)
Published as a *Pencil Points* cover in May 1925. In exhibitions of that year, this drawing was titled "The Clay Emerging into Practical Form." The vast scale of these setback cubes is indicated by one of HF's few representations of the human figure at the extreme lower left. The absence of people in his model metropolis has troubled various observers. See, for example, Lewis Mumford ("the eye detects not a single human being nor any provision for his wants") and Claude Brag-

don ("here is pictured a world from which humanity appears to have perished, done to death by its own egregious dream") in, respectively, *The New Republic*, Jan. 26, 1926, p. 271 and *The Frozen Fountain*, p. 33. From HF's viewpoint, however, the discrepancy between man and building in his imaginary city was merely an extrapolation of New York as he saw it each morning from his 18th floor penthouse studio at 101 Park Avenue (see *MT*, p. 16).

The Final Mass Carried Out in Steel (page 55)
First exhibited at the Anderson Galleries in 1925 and published in *The Sphere* of London (June 6, 1925, p. 293), this was one of HF's most influential renderings of the zoning law.

Glass (pages 56-57)
First published in *New York Times Magazine*, Mar. 21, 1926, p. 3, this drawing appeared in the "Machine-Age Exposition" of 1927, together with a Ferriss-designed model of a 35-story glass skyscraper that according to *The Christian Science Monitor* was the "outstanding novelty" of the show (Bibliography: Art Reviews). Both drawing and model may be seen in *The Graphic* of June 11, 1927, under the heading "The Crystal City of the Future." HF served as one of several directors of this exhibition and wrote an inspirational foreword for the illustrated catalog. For a related picture, see "Invisible Light Is Put to Work for Man," *The New York Times Magazine*, May 8, 1927, p. 4.

Lofty Terraces (pages 58-59)
Exhibited April 1925; and published as "Terraces under the Zoning Law," a *Pencil Points* cover illustration of June 1925; and as "The Family Upstairs," in *Vanity Fair*, "The New New York" (December 1925, pp. 66-67). For a related picture see "The Hanging Gardens of New York," *Literary Digest*, June 14, 1924, p. 31.

Imaginary Metropolis: Bird's-Eye View (page 60)
In the bustling and pragmatic '20s, HF pictured an ordered metropolis whose inhabitants "value emotion and mind equally with the senses" and in which three roughly corresponding "zones" of art, business, and science are disposed in such a way that all would share equally in the city's government. Each zone was to be dominated by a vast central tower surrounded by lower buildings, like foothills about a mountain.

The Art Center (page 61)
Like most of his contemporaries, HF was a great believer in the therapeutic properties of unlimited sunshine and fresh air, then much extolled by the medical profession.

The Business Center (pages 62-63)
The largest mountain of them all; almost exactly the height of the Empire State Building which at the time HF drew this picture was just getting underway (page 87).

The Science Center (pages 64-65)
This 1929 drawing, with its carefully placed jet of water in the foreground (springing from what appears to be a miniature skyscraper), calls to mind a stage set for some science fiction fantasy. Recent histories of American architecture point to the the reciprocal effect of stage and film design on the shape of many things, from radios to refrigerators (see Robinson and Bletter, *The Skyscraper Style*, pp. 10, 64).

Philosophy (pages 66-67)
HF's 1929 concept of unity in diversity was summed up in the final structure pictured in *MT*: a luminous tower based, like his city, upon a three-fold plan.

Proposal to Separate Pedestrian from Vehicular Traffic (pages 68-69)
These and the remaining drawings in this section originally appeared as a series of advertising illustrations for the American Institute of Steel Construction (AISC) in *The American Architect* (issues of April 1930 to March 1931) and in *Pencil Drawings of High Buildings and Bridges*, a brochure published by the AISC at about the same time. The three sketches shown here also appeared in *Creative Arts* of August 1931 (pp. 155-159) as "Examples of the Recent Work of Hugh Ferriss," with comment by the artist that is quoted in the caption. The original drawings were exhibited in the 1931 Architectural and Allied Arts Exposition at Grand Central Palace (see *New York Evening Post Gravure*, Apr. 18) and at the Roerich Museum show of 1932 (see Introduction, note 39, and Bibliography: Art Reviews).

Isolated Masses: Towers of Steel and Glass (pages 70-71)
AISC ad, *American Architect*, March 1931, p. 69; exhibited as above in 1932. (See illustration in *Pencil Points*, March 1932, p. 95.) The increased use of glass in steel-framed buildings allowed new freedom in design. This imaginary skyscraper also illustrates the shift from vertical to horizontal lines embodied in two actual examples of 1931: the McGraw-Hill Building, designed by Raymond Hood, and the Philadelphia Savings Fund Society Building (page 90) by Howe & Lescaze.

Mooring Mast: An Airport of the Future (pages 72-73)
Illustration in *American Architect*, August 1930, p. 67, and March 1932, p. 55 (a review of the Roerich Museum show). The artist's comment on this drawing (quoted in the caption from a penciled notation) no doubt was suggested by the "mooring mast" for dirigibles then under construction atop the Empire State Building, a few blocks downtown from his studio. Installation of the mast—greatly publicized at the time—required an unprecedented feat of construction. Landing machinery occupied 26 feet of space at the top of the spire, which was crowned by a "mooring ring," surrounded by warning lights, where the huge aircraft presumably would anchor. In fact, however, the only landing took place on the morning of September 16, 1931, when a privately owned dirigible piloted by William McCracken managed a three-minute connection with the mast in a stiff wind, a maneuver that brought Fifth Avenue traffic to a dead stop for half an hour.

Imaginary Seaport (pages 74-75)
AISC ad, *American Architect*, October 1930, p. 69: *The Architect*, December 1930, p. 104.

Skyscrapers Spanning Streets (page 76)
AISC ad, *American Architect*, April 1930, p. 69; also illustrated in Palmer Shannon, "Reproducing Architects' Renderings," *Architectural Record*, January 1931, p. 42; *New York Times Rotogravure*, Apr. 19, 1931 (a two-page picture); and *Creative Arts*, August 1931, p. 156.

Skyscraper Hangar in a Metropolis (page 77)
AISC ad, *American Architect*, January 1931, p. 69. HF's comment in the caption is from an interview on the day following the opening of his first one-man exhibition (*New York Times*, Apr. 14, 1925, p. 3). Here, two newly alighted passengers prepare for descent to a future city of multilevel traffic ways and widely spaced skyscrapers interspersed with low buildings crowned with gardens. Overhead a light airplane takes off; another swoops nonchalantly toward a landing "shelf" just wide enough to hold it. Though visions of this kind seem astonishingly naive today, it should be remembered that the airplane then was a new device of uncertain potentiality. It was not until Lindbergh's nonstop flight from New York to Paris in 1927 that American architects turned their thoughts to the design of air terminals and saw no reason not to locate them in the very heart of the city, just as Le Corbusier had done in his 1922 project for a "City of Three Million."

REALITIES, 1924–1968

American Radiator Building (page 80)
This drawing, titled "Spear-Points and Tom-Toms," appeared in Orrick John's article, "What the Modish Building Will Wear," *New York Times Magazine*, Oct. 4, 1925, p.11. The black-and-gold tower that Hood built for the American Radiator Company (now American Standard, Inc.), two years after the Chicago Tribune Building (page 82) launched him on his all-too-brief career, was an excellent example of what HF, in the '20s, most admired: an experimental spirit. Today, though newly gilded for the Bicentennial, the Radiator Building no longer provokes argument. People are oblivious to the plaque that proclaims this 20-story tower "an early instance of vivid coloration on the surface of the skyscraper," and have forgotten, if they ever knew, that Raymond Hood himself once made his headquarters on the 14th floor.

The Convocation Tower (page 81)
First exhibited in 1921, this drawing was reproduced in *MT* as HF's personal tribute to a much-admired architect of an older generation, Betram Grosvenor Goodhue (1869–1924), himself a master designer and draftsman. See also illustrations of this project in *Betram Grosvenor Goodhue*, edited by Charles Harris Whitaker (New York: Press of the American Institute of Architects, 1925), plates cxcvi and cxcvii.

Chicago Tribune Building (page 82)
This drawing appeared as an advertisement for the American Institute of Steel Construction in *Architect*, June 1927, p. 299.

The artist here took a characteristically even-handed stance midway between two warring groups led, on the one hand, by supporters of Hood's winning design for a 24-story Gothic tower (inspired, some said, by the ancient Tour du Beurre of Rouen Cathedral) and, on the other, by boosters of the second-prize entry, a relatively stark setback skyscraper put forward by the Finnish architect, Eliel Saarinen. As HF later noted, Hood's winning entry failed to influence subsequent building, while Saarinen, in losing the competition, provided inspiration to architects throughout this country (see, for example, The Chanin Building on page 85).

Chicago Board of Trade (page 83)
This drawing made its first public appearance in a 1928 exhibition at the Art Institute of Chicago and its most recent half a century later on the cover of a brochure published by the Commission on Chicago Historical and Architectural Landmarks to celebrate the naming of the Board of Trade Building as one of that select company. By that time, however, the original drawing had vanished without a trace.

The Shelton Hotel (Now the Halloran House) (page 84)
The drawing is a rear-view rendering of the completed building, first published in *The Architect*, April 1927, p. 21. For preliminary sketches and comment by the artist, see HF article, "A New Type of Building," *Christian Science Monitor*, Aug. 27, 1923, p. 7; also drawing of "The Shelton in Construction," *Pencil Points* cover, October 1923. One of the first and best results of the 1916 zoning law, this structure was greatly admired in the '20s as a straightforward manifestation of the new setback requirements.

The Chanin Building (page 85)
The drawing was commissioned in 1927 by the Chanin Corporation for reproduction on the cover of a handsome publicity brochure that proclaimed New York's newest skyscraper as the "*mise en scene* for the romantic drama of American business." Today, half a century later, this rendering is still in the hands of its original owners: a souvenir of that proud and hopeful era when the 56-story Chanin Building could still be regarded as "a national landmark . . . proof against all change forever."

The Chrysler Building (page 86)
This drawing was first published in *MT* when the Chrysler was still under construction. It is shown here just as a flag was hoisted at its summit signaling completion of the curved supports below. Although HF later regarded the Chrysler as a mausoleum that marked the end of an era (*PB*, p. 10), it appeared at the time as the height of fashion—a beguiling mixture of worldly Art Deco motifs imported from Paris and of American pizzazz strictly from Detroit. HF placed the Chrysler in his personal gallery of successful setbacks, because of the "extreme dimensions" of the great tower.

The Empire State Building (page 87)
The drawing appeared in *Architectural Forum*, June 1930 (plate 137, p. 787) a year before the building's completion.

When HF first projected the "sheer ascending planes" of the skyscraper then rising on the site of the old Waldorf-Astoria Hotel (see AISC ad, *Architecture*, September 1929, p. 34), it was still too early to predict what form the newcomer would take. John Jacob Raskob, its chief backer, had pictured a structure of 30 stories at most, but the spectacle of Walter Chrysler's ever-growing namesake on Lexington Avenue a few blocks south (page 86) caused him to raise his sights. By the time the building opened for business on May Day, 1931, it had soared to a record-breaking height of 102 stories and 1,250 feet, including the "mooring mast" (see pages 72–73), and had acquired a name of its own, the Empire State.

Daily News Building (pages 88–89)
The exterior view appears in *American Architect*, May 5, 1929, p. 588; *Architect and Building News*, July 26, 1929, p. 101; *Architectural Forum*, June 1930, p. 791; *Annual of American Design* (New York: Ives Washburn, 1931), p. 108. The Rotunda was drawn as an *MT* illustration (p. 39), and was published in *Architectural Forum*, November 1930, p. 551.

By way of contrast with the "small explosion of architectural effect" that Raymond Hood, in his words, provided for the lobby of the Daily News Building, the architect gave his masterwork a severely plain exterior that has made it a recognized precursor of the slab-shaped skyscrapers of later years.

Philadelphia Savings Fund Society Building (page 90)
"First Study of the Project, Now Under Construction," *Architectural Record*, April 1931, p. 306.

Lever House (page 91)
This drawing first appeared in *PB* and was a last-minute sketch of the just-completed building.

Preliminary Scheme for Rockefeller Center (pages 92–93)
See *The Building of the City*, Regional Plan Association of New York, pp. 112-115; and, "Examples of the Recent Work of Hugh Ferriss," *Creative Arts*, August 1931, pp. 154–159. These drawings were commissioned by Corbett, Harrison & MacMurray to illustrate early plans for Radio City (now Rockefeller Center), a site originally conceived as a home for the Metropolitan Opera but occupied after 1929 by Radio Corporation of America. The sketches subsequently were published by the Regional Plan Association of New York as illustrations for "A Proposed Art Center for Manhattan," a proposal that was to remain unrealized until the building of Lincoln Center (pages 98–99) 35 years later. In keeping with the Beaux-Arts background of the architects, this early plan has a strongly classical air. Even so, however, it requires only a slight effort of the imagination to see the basic elements of the present design: a broad entrance plaza, flanked by low structures that serve as intermediaries between Fifth Avenue and the looming skyscraper at the center of the composition, now the RCA building. The obelisk and arcades have been erased by time, to be sure, but the fountains are still very much in the foreground.

Eastern Airlines Building (pages 94–95)
The drawing recalls HF's 1926 visualization of glass buildings (pages 56–57). It was first reproduced in a Ferriss article, "Re Rendering," *Pencil Points*, July 1940.

General View, United Nations Headquarters (pages 96-97)
"Visualizing a Completed United Nations Site," *New York Times*, Oct. 23, 1949, p. 11. For additional published drawings by HF of the UN project see Introduction, notes 51, 54, and 55. See also Hales, *Architectural Rendering*, 10:35; Atkin, Corbelletti, and Fiore, *Pencil Techniques*, p. 87.

Lincoln Center for the Performing Arts (pages 98–99)
This preliminary sketch first appeared in the *New York Times Magazine*, May 25, 1958, p. 38. For a later overall view of the project, see feature articles, "The Lincoln Center Vision Takes Form," *New York Times Magazine*, Dec. 11, 1960, with illustration on pp. 8–9. With completion of Lincoln Center in 1968, New York's long-delayed dream of a cultural center became a reality at last. This romantic night view of the main plaza was projected by HF ten years earlier, a few months after the present 14-acre site was first established, but it shows an important trio of buildings very much as they appear today. The bronze horses silhouetted against the lighted archways of the Metropolitan Opera House never actually materialized, but were sketched by the artist as a tribute to the great equestrian statues of San Marco's Cathedral in Venice—just as the sphinxlike figures in the foreground of his zoning envelope studies of 35 years before (pages 62-63) had served as a fanciful salute to the "dateless spirit" of architecture.

Dams (pages 100–107)
Of all the structures that Ferriss chose to illustrate for his pictorial survey of "the power of America in buildings" in the summer and fall of 1941, the ones that appealed most powerfully to the artist himself were the great, government-built dams of the south and far west. Like the skyscrapers of Manhattan in the 1920s, they represented both a challenge and an opportunity to render, in dramatic terms, the basic mass of complex forms.

Norris (pages 100–101) and *Cherokee* (page 102) located, respectively, on the Clinch and Holston Rivers in Tennessee, are two of a series of large, main-river dams that were constructed in this region by the Tennessee Valley Authority between 1933 and 1944. At the time HF sketched them, a few months before Pearl Harbor, they were being made ready to supply power for the manufacture of munitions and atom bombs.

Hoover (page 103)—originally Boulder Dam from its location near Boulder City, Nevada—was the first large, multipurpose water project to be authorized (1928) by the federal government.

(Sketch published *New York Times Magazine*, Apr. 19, 1942.)

Grand Coulee (pages 104–105) and *Shasta* (pages 106–107), two more Bureau of Reclamation dams, were still under construction in 1941. (For published pictures of Grand Coulee, with comment by HF, see *New Pencil Points*, June 1942, pp. 59–60; September 1942, pp. 47–48.) At Grand Coulee, the largest of them all, two grandstands had been set up to allow the public a broad view of the spillway, but even from these vantage points it was difficult to grasp the magnitude of the subject or to realize that the power house, at lower right in the drawing, was equal in height to an 18-story building. For his first rough sketch, HF therefore chose a spot as near water level and as close under the power house as possible. "Now *that*," he shouted to a companion, above the water's roar, "is my idea of size!"

Red Rocks Park and Amphitheater (pages 108–111)

Looking back on his trip to this man-made amphitheater in the midst of the Rocky Mountains, HF later recalled that "these outcroppings of deep red rock are not only visually arresting but acoustically perfect. When Burnham Hoyt, the architect, stood down here one moonlit night, and I stood up yonder, I could readily hear his voice in conversational tone" (1948 speech, Beaux-Arts Architects). Hoyt and Ferriss may be seen, drawn to scale, on pages 110–111.

The Perisphere and Trylon during Construction (pages 112–113)

For illustrated references to HF's work on this project see *Architectural Forum*, May 1937, p. 390; *New York Times Magazine*, Oct. 23, 1938, pp. 6–7; *New York Times*, World's Fair Section, Mar. 5, 1939, pp. 4–5; *Pencil Points*, November 1936, pp. 613–615; *Perspecta*, vol. 13/14 (1971), p. 11.

The 1939 World's Fair was the product of two years' planning by a board of architects headed by Stephen F. Voorhees. As Design Consultant to the Board, it was HF's job to "note, study, and combine," through his drawings, plans put forward by members of the team. Of all his sketches and presentation renderings of the proposed theme structure, based on blueprints, diagrams, and models in a vast array of materials, none was more convincing than this study of the final result: an embodiment of the dramatic forms made possible by modern steel construction.

Factories (pages 114–117, 120–123)

A study in contrasts by three master architects. HF became acquainted with Albert Kahn on a visit to Detroit, not long before the famous industrial designer's death, and purposely chose, over better known examples, one of Kahn's smaller and earlier buildings, a steel foundry in Ohio (pages 120–121) to illustrate that architect's notable "lack of ostentation in allowing the facts to speak for themselves." The Ford Plant (pages 122–123) makes an interesting companion piece for Kahn's straightforward design.

The drawing on page 117 was one of a dozen renderings commissioned by General Motors and completed by HF during a stay of several weeks in 1945 at Cranbrook, Michigan, in consultation with the famous Finnish architect, Eliel Saarinen. The drawings were later exhibited in New York at the Waldorf-Astoria Hotel in 1945 as illustrations of GM's postwar building program and reproduced in *Eliel Saarinen* by Albert Christ-Janet (Chicago: The University of Chicago Press, 1948). After the elder Saarinen's death, the project was, in HF's words, "brilliantly carried out along revised lines" by his equally famous architect-son, Eero Saarinen.

After sketching the Johnson Wax Building (pages 114–116) in Racine, Wisconsin, HF and his family drove west to Madison for an overnight stay at Frank Lloyd Wright's home in Taliesin. Although the two men had met on several occasions since their first encounter in a radio broadcasting booth in 1929 (see Introduction, page 30), this was their first opportunity for an in-depth discussion about new developments in architecture, and HF requested Wright's advice in compiling his own list of outstanding American buildings. He was not altogether surprised to hear that *all* the recommended projects were designed by Frank Lloyd Wright himself.

Triborough Bridge Anchorage (page 124)

The architect's hand is unmistakable in this utilitarian structure, shown here in a rendering reminiscent of industrial images captured by photographer Margaret Bourke-White or painter Charles Sheeler.

Proposed Alterations, Metropolitan Museum of Art (page 125)

One of HF's more Piranesi-like drawings, commissioned by the architects of the proposed remodeling and now owned by the museum.

Bombproof Shelter (pages 128–129)

George J. Atwell, whose construction company, carried out excavation work for Rockefeller Center, among other large digging jobs, claimed that a tunnel 200 feet wide and 100 feet high could be drilled from the Hudson River through a mile and a half of solid stone to the Weehawken Meadows without diverting critical war materials, a proposal that was received with interest by President Franklin D. Roosevelt. These renderings were released to the press by Atwell on Dec. 7, 1942, the first anniversary of Pearl Harbor (*New York Sun*, Dec. 7, 1942; *New York Herald Tribune*, Dec. 8, 1942). In 1944, they won HF a prize for architectural drawing from The Architectural League of New York.

National Airport, Washington, D.C. (pages 130–131)

Published *New York Times Magazine*, Apr. 19, 1942, p. 9; also *New Pencil Points*, August 1942, pp. 71–72 (sketch and completed rendering, with comment by the artist).

BIBLIOGRAPHY

Other published references to Ferriss may be found in Notes for the Introduction. Biographical sources include the *American Architects Directory*, 1956; *Current Biography*, July 1945 and March 1962; *National Cyclopedia of American Biography*, 1927; *Who's Who in America*, 1928–1961; and *Who Was Who in America*, vol. 4 (1961–1968).

ART REVIEWS

A chronological list of published comment on exhibitions of Ferriss drawings in New York from 1925 to 1979. There is no attempt to list displays of the artist's work in cities other than New York or the numerous group shows in which his renderings have been included.

1925, "Drawings of the Future City"

First one-man show of 27 drawings at the Anderson Galleries, 489 Park Avenue at 59th Street. April 13–25.

American Art News, Apr. 18, p. 7.
Architect, July, p. 365.
Christian Science Monitor, Apr. 23, p. 8.
New York Evening Post, Apr. 18.
New York Times, Editorial, Apr. 14, III:2; Review, Apr. 18, IX, 11:2.
The Sphere (London), June 6.
Note: A selection of 20 drawings from this exhibition appeared late that year at the Print Club in Philadelphia and were reviewed in the *Philadelphia Enquirer* and *Record* on Oct. 25.

1925, "A Tercentenary Pictorial Pageant of New York"

Twelve mural-sized photographic enlargements of Ferriss drawings painted over in oils by the artist, were included in this large exhibition at John Wanamaker's Department Store. The series was entitled "A Vision of the Titan City, 1975." Opened Oct. 14.

Art News, Oct. 31, 1925, p. 10.
Mumford, Lewis, "The Sacred City." *New Republic*, Jan. 27, 1926.
New York Times, Oct. 14, 1925, p. 31; Oct. 21, 1925, p. 24.
Solon, Leon. "The Titan City Exhibition." *Architectural Record*, January 1926, pp. 92–94.

1926, "Solomon's Temple"

Project designed for the Philadelphia Sesquicentennial of 1926 by Corbett and Helmle, architects. Renderings with sketches and models by Corbett were exhibited at The Architectural League of New York (*New York Times*, Sept. 9, 1926, p. 6) and were included in a show of American architecture at the Berlin Academy of Fine Arts (catalog: Ausstellung Neuer Amerikanischer Baukunst, Akademie der Kunst zu Berlin, Januar 1926).

1927, Machine-Age Exposition.

Ferriss served as a director of this exhibition; he wrote an inspirational foreword to the catalog and exhibited two designs, one of which served as the basis for a model 35-story glass skyscraper, also featured in the show at 119 West 57th Street.

Christian Science Monitor, May 31, p. 7.
Graphic (London), June 11.

1932, "The Architectural Designs and Illustrations of Hugh Ferriss"

One-man show of 59 drawings at the Roerich Museum, 310 Riverside Drive at 103rd Street.

American Architect, March, p. 55.
Art Digest, Feb. 15, p. 6.
Christian Science Monitor, Feb. 18, p. 11.

New York Times, Feb. 7, II, 4:5; Feb. 13, p. 17.
Pencil Points, March, p. 95.

1942, "The Power of America in Buildings"
Fifty drawings at The Architectural League of New York.

New Pencil Points, June, p. 61.
New York Times, Apr. 19, p. 8. (For announcement of Brunner
    award for this project see the Times of Dec. 25, 1940.)

1942, "The Power of America in Buildings"
One-man show of 24 drawings at the Whitney Museum of American
Art.

Christian Science Monitor, May 16, p. 9.
Newsweek, May 11, p. 69.
New York Herald Tribune, May 5.
New York Times, May 5, p. 16; May 10, VIII, p. 5.
Studio Magazine, November, pp. 176–177.
Time, May 18, p. 42.
Travel, August, pp. 16–17.
Whitney Museum Bulletin, May 1.

1943, "American Industry at War"
Fifteen drawings in group show at Metropolitan Museum of Art.

New York Times, Mar. 5, p. 8; Mar. 14, II, p. 8.
Survey Graphic Magazine, May 1943, pp. 178–179.

1943, "Architectural Masses: A Group of Drawings by Hugh Ferriss"
Eighteen drawings and two photographic enlargements at the
American Academy of Arts and Letters.

New York Herald Tribune, May 16.
New York Times, May 14 (See also "Creative Artists Win $1,000
    Prizes," Apr. 14.)
New York World Telegram, May 15.

1953, "Power in Buildings"
Exhibition at Architectural League to coincide with publication of
book of the same name.

1962, Retrospective
Memorial exhibition at Architectural League.

1976, "Hugh Ferriss Drawings: An Architect's Vision"
Retrospective of 73 drawings at Gallery of Art, Steinberg Hall,
Washington University, St. Louis, Missouri. Illustrated catalog,
with introduction by Arline Leven.

Progressive Architecture, May, pp. 24–25.
St. Louis Post-Dispatch, Jan. 11.

Fourteen drawings from this exhibition appeared later that year at
the Century Club in New York. Comment by Walter Kilham.

1976, "America as Art"
Bicentennial exhibition at National Collection of Fine Arts, Smithsonian Institution, Washington, D.C. Four Ferriss drawings were
included in section entitled, "Image of Urban Optimism"; also illustrated in catalog and in publication prepared in conjunction with
this exhibition by the director, Joshua C. Taylor (see Books).

1976, "Architects for a New Nation, 1776–1976"
Two drawings included in exhibition of work in the collection of the
Avery Architectural Library, Columbia University, New York.
Catalog with comment by Avery Librarian Adolf K. Placzek.

Huxtable, Ada Louise. "The Revealing Art of Architectural Draw-
    ings." New York Times, Dec. 19.

1979, "Visionary Drawings: Architecture and Planning"
Five Ferriss drawings in group show at The Drawing Center. Illustrated catalog.

BOOK REVIEWS
The Metropolis of Tomorrow. New York: Ives Washburn, 1929.

American Architect, March 1930, p. 66.
American City, January 1930, p. 197.
Architecture, January 1930, pp. 47–48.
Brooklyn Eagle Magazine, Jan. 19, 1930, pp. 8–9.
Graphic (London), July 18, 1931, pp. 96–97.
New York Evening Post, 1929.
New York Herald Tribune, Jan. 19, 1930, Book Section, p. 1.
New York Times, Dec. 8, 1929, IV, 10:1.
Pencil Points, January 1930, p. 2.
Saturday Review of Literature: Woodbridge, Frederick J. "Plenty
    of Margin," Feb. 22, 1930, pp. 751–752. (See also comment in
    issue of Dec. 7, 1929, p. 542.)

Power in Buildings. New York: Columbia University Press, 1953.

Architectural Record, November 1953, p. 366.
Blake, Peter. "The Masonry Age." New York Times Book Review,
    Sept. 27, 1953.
Lippman, Herbert. "Union of Use and Beauty," Progressive Archi-
    tecture, December 1953, p. 166.
New York Herald Tribune, Dec. 27, 1953.
Scully, Vincent. Art in America, October 1954, p. 232.
Tintner, Adeline R. Art Digest, Nov. 1, p. 25.
Zucker, Paul. Journal of Aesthetics and Art Criticism, June 1954.

BOOKS
With illustrations by Hugh Ferriss and/or comment on his work.

Adams, Thomas. *The Building of the City.* Vol. 2, *Regional Plan
of New York and Its Environs.* New York: Committee on Regional
Plan, 1931.

Atkin, William W.; Corbelletti, Raniero; and Fiore, Vincent R.
Pencil Techniques in Modern Design. New York: Reinhold, 1953.

———. *The Arch Lectures.* New York: Creative Age Press, 1942.

Bossom, Arthur. *Building to the Skies: The Romance of the Skyscraper.* London: Studio Ltd., 1934.

Bragdon, Claude. *The Frozen Fountain: Essays on Architecture.*
New York: Alfred A. Knopf, 1932.

Burchard, John, and Bush-Brown, Albert. *The Architecture of
America: A Social and Cultural History.* Boston: Atlantic Monthly
Press Book; Little, Brown & Co., 1961.

Cheney, Sheldon. *The New World Architecture.* New York: Long-
mans, Green & Co., 1930.

Clute, Eugene. *Drafting Room Practice.* New York: The Pencil
Points Press, 1928.

Conrads, Ulrich, and Sperlich, Hans G. *The Architecture of Fantasy.* New York: Praeger, 1962.

Edgell, G.H. *The American Architecture of Today.* New York:
Charles Scribner's Sons, 1928.

Farey, Cyril Arthur. *Architectural Drawing, Perspective and Rendering.* New York: Charles Scribner's Sons, 1931.

Ferriss, Hugh. *The Metropolis of Tomorrow.* New York: Ives Washburn, 1929.

———. *Power in Buildings*. New York: Columbia University Press, 1953.

Fitch, James Marston. *American Building: The Forces That Shape It*. Boston: Houghton Mifflin Co., 1948.

Guptill, Arthur L. *Sketching and Rendering in Pencil*. New York: The Pencil Points Press, Inc., 1929.

Halse, Albert. *Architectural Rendering*. New York: F. W. Dodge, Corp., 1969.

Hamlin, Talbot. *The American Spirit in Architecture*. New Haven, Conn.: Yale University Press, 1926.

Hitchcock, Henry-Russell. *Modern Architecture, Romanticism and Reintegration*. New York: Payson & Clarke Ltd., 1929.

Huxtable, Ada Louise. *Kicked a Building Lately?* New York: Quadrangle/The New York Times Book Company, 1976.

Jordy, William H. *American Buildings and Their Architects*. Vol. 4, *The Impact of European Modernism in the Mid-Twentieth Century*. New York: Doubleday, 1972.

Kidney, Walter C. *The Architecture of Choice: Eclecticism in America, 1880–1930*. New York: Braziller, 1974.

Kilham, Walter H., Jr. *Raymond Hood, Architect: Form through Function in the American Skyscraper*. New York: Architectural Book Publishing Company, 1973.

Kimball, Fiske. *American Architecture*. Indianapolis, Ind.: The Bobbs-Merrill Co., 1928.

Koolhaas, Rem. *Delirious New York*. New York: Oxford University Press, 1978.

Mujica, Francisco. *History of the Skyscraper*. Paris: Archeology and Architectural Press, 1929.

Robinson, Cervin, and Bletter, Rosemarie Haag. *The Skyscraper Style: Art Deco, New York*. New York: Oxford University Press, 1975.

Scully, Vincent. *American Architecture and Urbanism*. New York: Praeger, 1969.

Sexton, Randolf Williams. *American Commercial Buildings of Today*. New York: Architectural Book Publishing Co., 1928.

———. *The Logic of Modern Architecture*. New York: Architectural Book Publishing Co., 1929.

Stone, Michelle, and Sky, Alison. *Unbuilt America: Forgotten Architecture in the United States from Thomas Jefferson to the Space Age*. New York: McGraw-Hill, 1976.

Taylor, Joshua C. *America as Art*. Washington, D.C.: Smithsonian Institution Press, 1976. *(See* Art Reviews, 1976.)

Wattjes, J.G. *Moderne Architectuur*. Amsterdam: Kosmos, 1927.

Willis, Carol. "The Early Work of Hugh Ferriss." Unpublished Masters thesis, Columbia University, 1976.

Wolf, Peter. *The Future of the City: New Directions in Urban Planning*. New York: Whitney Library of Design, 1974.

ARTICLES AND PUBLISHED TALKS ON RENDERING AND ARCHITECTURAL DESIGN: 1921–1955

In chronological order.

On Rendering

"Three Stages of a Rendering." *Pencil Points*, January 1921, pp. 6–9, 36. Subject: Bush House, London. Helmle & Corbett, Architects.

"Truth in Architectural Rendering" (Talk). *American Institute of Architects Journal*, March 1925, pp. 99–101. Also reprinted as a brochure by The Architectural League of New York. For comment see: Leon Solon, "A Notable Discussion on Rendering," *Architectural Record*, June 1925.

"On Drawings of Buildings." *New York Times*, April 23, 1925, 16:1.

"On Architectural Rendering" (Talk). *Christian Science Monitor*, Apr. 30, 1925, p. 5.

"Rendering, Architectural." *The Encyclopaedia Britannica*, 1929–1973 (revised version after 1961, titled "Architectural Rendering").

"How Hugh Ferriss Draws: Six Stages of a Rendering." *American Architect*, July 1931, pp. 30–33.

"Re Renderings." *Pencil Points*, July 1940, pp. 400–403.

On Architectural Design

"The New Architecture." *New York Times Book Review* and *Magazine*, Mar. 19, 1922, p. 8.

"Civic Architecture of the Immediate Future." *Arts and Decoration*, November 1922, pp. 12–13.

"Cubes and Pyramids." *Christian Science Monitor*, Oct. 8, 1923, p. 7.

"New York from a Studio Rooftop." *Christian Science Monitor*, December 1923, p. 7.

"Scene: New York Time: Now: The Unfinished Drama of the Modern Metropolis." *Theatre Guild Magazine*, May 1929.

Foreword, Catalog for Machine-Age Exposition of 1927. *(See* Art Reviews.)

"Frank Lloyd Wright and Hugh Ferriss Discuss This Modern Architecture" (Reprint of a radio broadcast). *Architectural Forum*, November 1930, p. 537.

"Examples of the Recent Work of Hugh Ferriss" (Text cover drawing, futuristic designs). *Creative Arts*, August 1931, pp. 155–159, 164–165.

"The Real Traditions of Architecture." *Annual of American Design*, 1936.

"Power of America" (Talk). *The New Pencil Points*, June 1942, pp. 59–62.

"Architecture with Two Legs" (Talk). *AIA Journal*, May 1945, pp. 171–174.

"Designing the United Nations Headquarters" (Talk). *Journal of the Royal Architectural Institute of Canada*, March 1948, pp. 69–80.

"Words to an Art Commission" (Talk). *AIA Journal*, May 1948, pp. 195–200.

"New York in 1999." *New York Times*, Feb. 6, 1949, pp. 18–19.

"Architecture Now" (Talk). *AIA Journal*, April 1951, pp. 163–169.

"The Next Step in Design: A Synthesis of Technology and Vision" (Talk). *AIA Journal*, August 1952, pp. 60–66. See also *Architectural Record*, August 1952, p. 11.

"The Impact of Scientific Materialism on Art Today" (Talk). *AIA Journal*, July 1954, pp. 3–6.

"Time for an Artistic Revival in Architectural Design" (Talk). *AIA Journal*, Feb. 1955, pp. 51–57. Also *Architectural Forum*, March 1955, pp. 143.

A SUPPLEMENTARY LIST OF PUBLISHED DRAWINGS

The list is divided into three sections, *General Illustrations*, *Architectural Trends*, and *Building Projects*, and the entries under each heading are arranged in chronological order. Listing by picture title alone indicates one or more illustrations accompanied by little or no text; by author's name, an article with several illustrations by HF and comment on his work. Additional references to published work by the artist may be found in the Notes for the Introduction and the Drawings reproduced in this book.

General Illustrations

"Vie de Bohême in Washington Square: Sketches by H. and D. Ferriss." *Vanity Fair*, August 1915, p. 36.

Four Cathedralesque Churches in New York: Sketches by Hugh Ferriss. *Vanity Fair*.

"Two on a Bus: Glimpses of Fifth Avenue from the Top of a Pea-Green Stage." *Vanity Fair*, March 1916, p. 60.

St. Louis sketches. *St. Louis, Post-Dispatch*, March 12 and 19, 1916.

"On the Road to Mandalay—at the Ritz: The New Luncheon and Tea House at the Ritz-Carleton in New York" (Warren & Wetmore, designers). *Vanity Fair*, July 1916.

"Washington Square Arch." Cover of *The Quill* magazine of Greenwich Village, October 1917.

"Varied Types of New York Clubs." *Vanity Fair*, October 1917, p. 72.

"Two Recent Architectural Successes: The Bush Building and the Greenwich Village Theatre." *Vanity Fair*, November 1917, p. 69.

"The New Heart of Bohemia: New York's Smock Colony Settles in Sheridan Square." *Vanity Fair*, January 1918, p. 50.

"The 'Tuckahoe,' Just 27 Days from Keel Laying to Launching." Cover of magazine section, *The World*, June 2, 1918.

"Rush Order Work on America's New Merchant Navy." Five ship construction drawings, *The World*, July 9, 1918, pp. 8–9.

"Fourth of July Parade, Convoyed by Airplanes, Passing the Public Library." *New York Herald Tribune*, July 14, 1918. (See also edi-torial comment on the drawing in *Reedy's Mirror*, St. Louis, July 19, 1918; note that this drawing has been added to recent acquisitions in the print division of the New York Public Library, *The World*, Aug. 4, 1918.)

Brown, Frank Chouteau. "A New Note in Architectural Rendering: The Work of Mr. Hugh Ferriss." *Architectural Review* (Boston), August 1918, pp. 21–25. (First appreciation of HF's work; 10 sketches, 6 full-page plates.)

"New York in Wartime: A Sudden and Picturesque Transformation." *Vanity Fair*, October 1918, pp. 54–55.

"The Avenue of the Allies." *Vanity Fair*, November 1918, p. 34.

"American Capitals of Industry." *Harper's Magazine*, July 1919, pp. 217–224.

"The New Fifth Avenue Plaza at Night." *Vanity Fair*, February 1922, p. 28.

"Jefferson Market, New York City." *Pencil Points*, January 1923, plate II.

"The Birthplace of James Fenimore Cooper, Burlington, New Jersey." *Christian Science Monitor*, Sept. 14, 1923, p. 6.

Ferriss, Hugh. "House-Hunting in Bermuda." *Christian Science Monitor*, February 1924.

"New Year's Eve in New York" (design for a stage set, a Theatre Guild production by Werner Janssen at the Mecca Auditorium, New York). *Theatre Guild Magazine*, March 1930, p. 28.

"The 481-foot-high Pyramid of Cheops as Hugh Ferriss Imagines It Would Look in Central Park" (A suggestion by architect L. Andrew Reinhard). *Architectural Forum*, January 1934, p. 24.

"Super Salvage Job" [The U.S.S. Lafayette (Normandie) in salvage process after a fire]. *New York Times Magazine*, Sept. 6, 1942, pp. 16-17.

"A Proposal for St. Louis of the Future." Editorial comment and drawings commissioned by the *St. Louis Post-Dispatch*, May 28, 1950.

Architectural Trends

Price, C. Matlock. "The Trend of Architectural Thought in America." *Century Magazine*, September 1921, pp. 709–722 (small sketches of assorted buildings in New York, St. Louis, Texas.)

Corbett, Harvey Wiley. "Zoning and the Envelope of the Building." *Pencil Points*, April 1923, pp. 15–18.

"Architectural Tendencies of Today: Five Recent Examples Drawn by Hugh Ferriss." *Vanity Fair*, February 1924, pp. 44–45.

"The Hanging Gardens of Babylon: A Vision of What the Future May or May Not Bring." *Literary Digest*, June 14, 1924, p. 31.

Johns, Orrick. "The Excelsior of Architecture." *New York Times Magazine*, July 20, 1924, p. 3 (Illustration: "Ascending Scale").

———. "What the Well-Dressed Building Will Wear." *New York Times Magazine*, Dec. 28, 1924, p. 10 (Illustration: "A City of Needles").

Ciolkowska, Muriel. "Hugh Ferriss and the Zoning Laws of New York." *Architectural Review* (London), November 1925, pp. 174–177.

Sorgel, Herman. "Hugh Ferriss." *Baukunst*, January 1926, pp. 18ff (22 zoning law illustrations, editorial comment, reprint of HF's 1923, "Cubes and Pyramids" from *The Christian Science Monitor*; see articles by HF).

"City Planner, Poet, Differ on Beauty of Skyscraper" (Hugh Ferriss and Lola Ridge, poet and editor, discuss the city on an excursion ferry around Manhattan). *The World*, Editorial Section, June 1, 1930 (photo).

"Ferriss's Future-Perfect." *Time*, May 18, 1942, pp. 42–43 [comment on the Whitney Museum exhibition (see Art Reviews), with portrait and illustrated review of the artist's career].

Zoll, Stephen. "Superville: New York Aspects of Very High Bulk." Monograph published by the *Massachusetts Review*, Summer, 1973, vol. 14, pp. 447–539 (illustrations from *MT*, with comment).

Huxtable, Ada Louise. "Looking Back at the World of Tomorrow." *New York Times Magazine*, January 1975, pp. 40–43 (a retrospective view of HF, with illustrations).

Tafuri, Manfredo, "Vie et Mort du Gratte-ciel." *L'Architecture d'Aujourd'hui*, March-April, 1975 (Illustrations by HF, with comment, on pp. 6, 15, 58–59).

Building Projects

Chicago

Adler Planetarium (Ernest A. Grunsfeld, Jr., Architect). *Pencil Points*, October 1929, p. 698.

Chicago Exposition, 1933:
The Ford Motor Building. *Design Magazine*, June 1934, pp. 18-19.
"Tower of Water and Light" (Voorhees, Gmelin & Walker, Architects). Illustration for article, "The Committee for the Preservation of Architectural Records Moves On," *Architectural Record*, August 1979, pp. 78–79.

Detroit

Detroit branch of the Chicago Federal Reserve Bank (Graham, Anderson, Probst & White, Architects). *Architects*, December 1927, p. 302.

Detroit Public Library (Cass Gilbert, Architect). *Pencil Points*, December 1927, p. 751.

Note: These drawings were commissioned in 1927 by Hudson's Department Store in Detroit, as part of a series on city landmarks. Other subjects included were the Fisher Building, Albert Kahn, Architect; the Penobscot Building, Smith, Hinchman & Grylls, Architects; and the Stott Building, Donaldson & Meier, Architects. HF studies of this trio of Detroit skyscrapers may be seen in *MT*.

Kansas City

Kansas City War Memorial (H. Van Buren Magonigle, Architect). *Western Architect*, October 1926, p. 128.

New York

The Woolworth Building. *Literary Digest*, Oct. 23, 1920, p. 76 (advertising drawing for National Terra Cotta Society).

"The Fine New Playhouse of the Theatre Guild: Advance Sketches by Hugh Ferriss" (C. Howard Crane, Architect; Norman Bel-Geddes, consultant). *Vanity Fair*, August 1924, p. 32.

Apartment building, 24 West 40 Street, (Ely Jacques Kahn, Architect). *Pencil Points*, December 1924, plate XLV, pp. 51ff.

"A Selection of Drawings of Works by the Late Donn Barber" (illustration of the "Proposed Broadway Temple in New York City"). *Pencil Points*, December 1925, p. 78.

"Vanity Fair's New Home—The Graybar Building: The Largest Office Building in the World." *Vanity Fair*, March 1927, p. 77.

Bank of Manhattan Building; "Proposed New York Regional Plan Limitations on Building Bulk" (H. Craig Severance, Inc., Architects & Engineers; Yasuo Matsui, Associate Architect). *Architectural Record*, February 1932, p. 38.

Cathedral of St. John the Divine. *Pencil Points*, June 1938.

Hayden Planetarium, Museum of Natural History (Trowbridge & Livingston, Architects). *Architecture* (London), vol. 73 (1943), p. 133.

Idlewild: "Finest Airport in the World." *New York Times Magazine*, Jan. 21, 1945, pp. 10-11.

The Unisphere: Symbol of the 1964–65 World's Fair (photo of Robert Moses, president of the fair, inspecting HF's drawing).

Philadelphia

Sales Building, Packard Motor Car Company of Philadelphia (Albert Kahn, architect). *Pencil Points*, June 1921, p. 43.

"The Sesqui-Centennial at Philadelphia: An Artist's Impressions of the Exposition Buildings." *Vanity Fair*, July 1926, pp. 46–47.

"U.S. Post Office and Court House, Philadelphia" (design by Harry Sternfeld and the Ballinger Company; (this drawing won the artist a Birch Burdette Long Memorial Prize for architectural draftsmanship from The Architectural League). *Pencil Points*, May 1934, pp. 208, 210; *Architectural Forum*, June 1934, p. 34; *Design*, September 1935, pp. 23, 33.

St. Louis

"Federal Reserve Bank of St. Louis" (Mauran, Russell & Crowell, Architects). *American Architect*, July 18, 1923, p. 60.

Southwestern Bell Telephone Company Building. "Southwestern Bell Telephone Company: Final Study of Mass." *Pencil Points*, December 1924, cover. *Architectural Record*, June 1925, pp. 574–576. (See also "Administration and Equipment Building," *Pencil Points*, October 1925, cover. This drawing was reprinted as an AISC advertisement in *Architect*, March 1927, p. 679.)

San Francisco

Pacific Edgewater Club, Point Lobos (Milton Pflueger, Architect). *American Architect*, June 20, 1927, p. 823.

San Francisco Stock Exchange (winning design; J.R. Miller and T.L. Pflueger, Architects). *Pencil Points*, April 1928, p. 237.

West Virginia

West Virginia State Capitol (Cass Gilbert, Architect). *Pencil Points*, May 1923, cover.

PHOTOGRAPHY CREDITS

Edited by Sharon Lee Ryder and Susan Davis
Designed by Jay Anning
Graphic production by Ellen Greene
Set in 14 point Bodoni Book